The
Word of God
With
Power

Other books by Jack Taylor

Prayer: Life's Limitless Reach
The Key to Triumphant Living
The Hallelujah Factor
God's Miraculous Plan of Economy

The Word of God *With* Power

Experiencing the Full Meaning and Blessing of the "Word of God"

Jack R. Taylor

BROADMAN
& HOLMAN
PUBLISHERS

Nashville, Tennessee

4260-87
ISBN: 0-8054-6087-X

Dewey Decimal Classification: 220
Subject Heading: BIBLE // DOCTRINAL THEOLOGY
Library of Congress Card Catalog Number: 93-22891
Printed in the United States of America

Unless otherwise stated,
all Scripture quotations are from the Holy Bible, *King James Version*. Scripture
quotations marked (NIV) are from the Holy Bible, *New International Version,*
copyright 1973, 1978, 1984 by International Bible Society; (NEB) from the *New
English Bible*, copyright © The Delegates of the Oxford University Press and the
Syndics of the Cambridge University Press, 1961, 1970, reprinted by
permission; and (TLB) *The Living Bible*, copyright © Tyndale House Publishers,
Wheaton, Illinois, 1971, used by permission.

Library of Congress Cataloging-in-Publication Data
Taylor, Jack R.
The word of God with power : experiencing the full meaning and blessing of the
"Word of God" / Jack Taylor.
p. cm.
Includes bibliographical references.
ISBN 0-8054-6087-X
1. Bible—Evidences, authority, etc. 2. Bible—Inspiration. 3. Reformed Church—
Doctrines. 4. Evangelicalism. I. Title.
BS480.T39 1993
220.1—dc20c20   93-22891
                                                                                     CIP

Table of Contents

Luke 1:37

King James Version
"For with God nothing shall be impossible."

Literal Greek to English
"No word from God is without dynamic."

Negative to Positive
"Every word from God is powerful."

ॐ

Luke 4:32

"And they were astonished at his doctrine:
for his word was with power."

ॐ

Hebrews 4:12

King James Version
"For the word of God is quick, and powerful."

Personal Paraphrase
"For the word of God is alive and full of energy."

Literal from Greek
"Living is the word of God and operative."

ॐ

1 Corinthians 1:18

King James Version
"For the preaching of the cross is to them that perish foolish-
ness; but unto us which are saved it is the power of God."

Literal Translation
"For the word of the cross . . . is the power of God."

ॐ

Acknowledgments

To Jamie Buckingham and Jim Mahoney, whose illnesses were the launching pads for this study and whose lives were miraculously extended by the sheer power of the Word of God.

To those along the way who read the partial manuscript, made valuable suggestions, and provided great encouragement: Luther Dyer, Joe Johnson, Bob Mumford, Tom Clark, Bill Jaggar, and Ron Lentine.

To De Verne Fromke, who early in the formative stages of these concepts, said, "Jack, the church must hear this message." That was a needed shove.

To thousands who have heard me haltingly share these life-altering principles and cheered me on.

Thank you, one and all. Please receive this work with trust that a *great awakening* will soon break over us all!

A Strange Suggestion?
Read the Last Chapter First!

The traveler generally has foremost in his or her mind the destination. All the sights along the way may be interesting, but the destination shapes the perspective.

When a boy, Vance Havner read adventure novels. He reported that he always read the last chapter first, a method of avoiding needless stress during the thickening plot in the middle chapters. Thus when the villain was gaining ground and his malignant plans seemed about to succeed, Vance could confidently whisper, "Now, Mr. Villain, I have read the last chapter and you don't make it to the end!" A good practice!

You might try that here, with the postscript which begins on page 177. The final perspective should color the whole journey.

&

Perspective

I have never had a serious question, even for one moment, about the Bible's complete reliability as the Word of God. At first, this freedom from doubt may have been the result of blissful ignorance and child-like naivete. I simply did not have a doubtful mentality. I even believed that the mail-order catalogs were reliable. Time after time, as we did much of our shopping from far out in the country, those amazing source books unerringly "delivered the goods." If Sears and Roebuck and Montgomery Ward were deserving of our faith, I joyfully assumed that I had no reason to be suspicious about the claims of the Bible. It too has delivered the goods.

In retrospect, I remember no time when I placed the Bible in a position where my mind had the kind of authority to question it. The Bible always has been above my mind, not below it. When I was saved at the age of ten, my respect for the Bible was wonderfully confirmed. What a Book! Its simple message promising salvation was proven in my life! Its impact was demonstrated to be the "power of God unto salvation."

When I was called to preach at fourteen, it never occurred to me that God had anything in mind for me except the declaration of the Bible's truths. Not until I was in a seminary was I even aware anyone considered himself wise enough to question it. I was under the impression before then that what God had to say in the Bible was far above anyone's ability to question. In fact I was shocked to know that thinking people put themselves up as its critics. I thought I was chosen to *preach* it, not *question* it or *criticize* it.

I heard nothing in my seminary training that led me to believe my professors had any doubt about the Book which comprised the heart of their curricula. I was under the impression that if there were such folks on the planet who doubted the Bible as God's Word they were far, far away. But these strange phantoms were often referred to as liberals: those who had doubts about the authenticity and reliability of the Book which I so deeply respected.

In the sixties much of the theological world entered again upon the ancient battlefield of the historicity of the Bible's first five books and their Mosaic authorship. The bitter battle peaked in the firing of a seminary professor who had advocated in his book that Genesis was not historical but allegorical. During the ensuing years there were regional battles and institutional squabbles but nothing of national consequence.

In the late seventies the rumblings of discontent came to the surface, and we were ushered again into war over the beloved Book. Lines were drawn. Phrases were coined which separated brother from brother and sister from sister. I felt anger, frustration, and discomfort. I watched as strategies were drawn up to win back the Bible's place of respect it surely deserved.

With each passing year for more than a decade, it was hoped that the battle was over. But with each year it seemed to escalate. "Inerrancy" seemed to become the password. Without the password there was no admission into the fellowship of the conservative cause. I was chagrined, not because I was an inerrantist, but because there were those who were not. Surely we were fighting an imagined phantom. I agreed with the rhetoric of the conservative cause. Yes, the Bible was completely reliable, replete with the revelation of God and His Christ as He intended it. Yes, the Scriptures were without error in the "original autographs."

I found myself in a strange position. I believed with all my heart in the reliability of the Bible. I willingly embraced all the words used to describe it, including "inerrant." But I was not comfortable with the crossfire. I found myself strangely aloof from either position. I refused to *debate* what I had been called to *declare*.

Now, at least for a time, the battle seems to have subsided somewhat, and Christians of all persuasions have divided somewhat. There is a peace, albeit uneasy and tenuous. Every now and again the cease-fire is broken, and a volley explodes across the battlefield, now strewn with casualties.

In the midst of the struggle, I experienced an extended illness and hospitalization. This afforded me a time when I could step back far enough and long enough to get a perspective I might not otherwise have gotten. I asked myself questions that I had seldom considered before.

What does it mean that the Bible is the Word of God? Did God give us the Bible and choose to be silent afterward? Does the Bible really need our defense or does it demand our declaring of it? What are the issues behind the issues?

As I began the search for answers, I heard within myself my own "distant rumblings." I was laid up for over one hundred days with little to do but to read the Bible, listen to God, and let Him renew my broken body, weakened by a life-threatening illness and violated by three serious surgeries. As the healing slowly and painfully progressed, something also began to happen in my spirit.

What you are about to read is what I believe I began to hear from God during those crisis days. This is not a book about inerrancy. It is about something *beyond inerrancy*. It is transcendent to inerrancy. It involves what I call "truth at the edge."

Several of our faith's most vital truths lie at the border or edge of the great body of truths that make up our belief system. Just past these truths lies heresy. For that reason we must practice great care and precision in accepting and expressing these truths. I assure you that I have read and rearranged, edited and deleted, and toned down and clarified more in this manuscript than in any book I have written. Several statements, while true, sounded harsh. I changed them. Others were just too close to the edge; unsuspecting folks might have read them and "fallen off." I deleted these statements. Still others seemed on the surface to depreciate the greatest Book that ever existed, the Bible. I sought to clarify these. I may have missed a few that will give readers a problem. I have sought to deal with issues and not with people. Any reference to a persuasion or a position is for illustration and nothing more.

I have not been known in recent years for being particularly careful of man-made boundaries. When a truth is discovered, I perceive it to be for the *whole* body of Christ. These truths are for all, not just Baptists, Methodists, Charismatics, Pentecostals, Presbyterians, Episcopalians, Nazarenes, Mennonites, Adventists, Catholics, Independents, Brethren, but for *all*! (Sorry if I left you out.) I joyfully commit myself to reach across arbitrary borders to interact with those of "a different stripe."

I have always said, "I'm a lover, not a fighter." I do not fight well. My constitution is not made for controversy. I would rather have a prayer meeting than a debate. I believe more is accomplished in a foot-washing than in a wrestling match. I can love anybody who loves Jesus, oddities notwithstanding. I do not do well when Christians get mean, when saints behave "unsaintly."

The realm that occupies this book's subject matter lies out on "the edges." Some things here are bound to disturb the narrow comfort zone of traditional evangelicalism. I have been and remain an inerrantist, as I understand inerrancy. I believe that a high view of Scripture is absolutely necessary to admission into this transcendent realm. Because I believe this, I will devote the first chapter to the subject of "inerrancy." We will not likely get *beyond* it unless and until we *reach it* and *go through* it.

After that we shall move into the realm beyond inerrancy, the Word of God with power.

In Defense of Power

"Power" is not an evil word; it is an inevitable issue. We see it throughout the universe; we encounter it in every realm of thought.

Power, next to holiness, is the church's greatest need today. Power without holiness is destructive; holiness without power is dead. We must have both. Though wounded in its friends' house and abused by extremists, power in the church is a crying need.

The source of all power is the Word of God. He created everything by His own Word. The Genesis record is replete with the power of God's spoken Word creating light, matter, life, energy, and time. This shows that the Word of God is the power source of the universe. From the womb of the Word came forth everything that is. Without the Word nothing was created. This is the great cosmic premise.

This book is about the Word of God in its widest meaning. Though written in a book, God's Word in its fullest definition cannot be confined to a document. The value of the document, the Bible, is increased, not decreased by this recognition.

In all references in these pages to the Bible, "Word" is capitalized to indicate its value and standing as part of God. We are accustomed to the capitalization of the word "Scripture." We do well to be consistent by doing the same with the Word of God in its widest usage.

Too many Scripture references connect the Word of God and power for us to disregard this vital union. Though they are dealt with in the following pages, it is appropriate to preview a few here:

> I am not ashamed of the gospel of Christ: for it is the *power* of God unto salvation to every one that believeth.
> —Romans 1:16 (emphasis added)

> And upholding all things by the word of his *power.*
> —Hebrews 1:3 (emphasis added)

> The word of God is quick [alive], and *powerful.*
> —Hebrews 4:12 (emphasis added)

> The preaching [Word] of the cross is to them that perish foolishness; but unto us which are saved it is the *power* of God.
> —1 Corinthians 1:18 (emphasis added)

> They were astonished at his doctrine: for his word was with [authority and] *power.*
> —Luke 4:32 (emphasis added)

Other passages refer to the power of God's Word in the creation, sustaining, and the consummation of the universe.

> Through faith we understand that the worlds were framed by the word of God.
> —Hebrews 11:3

He spake, and it was done;
he commanded, and it stood steadfast.
—Psalm 33:9

So shall my word be that goeth forth out of my mouth: it shall
not return unto me void, but it shall accomplish that which I
please, and it shall prosper in the thing whereto I sent it.
—Isaiah 55:11

These Scriptures make clear that in the Word of God is the greatest
force in existence, the power of God Himself. In view of the seem-
ing abuse of power and the reaction to it, we are in danger of com-
mitting an equal error—disregarding the desperate need for power
in the church today. I make no apology for the title and repeated
emphases on the aspect of power and the Word of God.

When the church was a "babe," holiness was its trademark. One
day soon she will be a "bride" adorned with holiness *and* power.
The Word of God mandates the fulfillment of her destiny. God's
Word will return to Him having accomplished His desires and purpose.

"Blessed are those who are invited to the wedding supper of the
Lamb!" . . . I saw heaven standing open and there before me was
a white horse, whose rider is called Faithful and True. With jus-
tice he judges and makes war. His eyes are like blazing fire, and
on his head are many crowns. He has a name written on him
that no one knows but he himself. He is dressed in a robe
dipped in blood, and his name is *the Word of God*. The armies of
heaven were following him, riding on white horses and dressed
in fine linen, white and clean. Out of his mouth comes a sharp
sword with which to strike down the nations. "He will rule with
an iron scepter." He treads the winepress of the fury of the wrath
of God Almighty. On his robe and on his thigh he has this name
written: KING OF KINGS AND LORD OF LORDS.
—Revelation 19:9, 11-16, NIV

An awesome display of power, wouldn't you say?
The Word of God has power! I rest my case.

—Jack R. Taylor

੨੪

*In every generation
the integrity of the Bible is called into question.
The debates,
while differing in details and persons,
line up in similar manner.
The results are generally the same:
there is agreement to disagree, sometimes disagreeably,
with friends separating and schisms established
in the body of Christ.
We again learn from history
that we learn little from history.
It is well, however, to back up from the present furor
and take a look at history.*

—JRT

Chapter 1

Examining Biblical Inerrancy

In the summer of 1520 Martin Luther delivered his famous "Address to the Nobility of the German Nation." In it he blasted the idea that the popes were lords of Scripture and could not err in faith. Four and a half centuries later the evangelical community is embattled, not over the infallibility of popes or indeed the infallibility of the Scriptures (in the classical understanding of that phrase), but rather over the infallibility of the word "inerrancy" to describe the total authority and credibility of the Scripture in its original form.[1]

The inerrancy debate is not new, and great men of faith have long taken their stands on either side. A prominent case is that of B. B. Warfield and G. C. Berkhouwer. Warfield was aggressively committed to the strictest idea of inerrancy. Berkhouwer, on the other hand, while equally committed to the reliability of the Scriptures, was uncomfortable with the strict use of inerrancy.

It seems that in every era in which the debate resurfaces the margins for tolerance on both sides tend to shrink. Often in times of heated theological debate, overstatements are made on either side.

One such statement claims the Scriptures were dictated word for word, leaving no risk of mistake because it did not pass through the authors' minds. This certainly is not the claim of inerrancy, nor is it safe ground on which to stand.

Inerrancy is *not* certain other things:

It is not the claim that any version is without error. If this were the case, the war would be over the versions, not just inerrancy.

It is not the claim that the science and geography statements are flawless. It is needless to try to "take up for the Bible" when it makes statements that appear to fly in the face of recognized scientific truths. The Bible does not claim to be a scientific book. Those who wrote it were not scientists or geographers, nor do their statements detract from the mystery and majesty of the Bible as the Book on humankind's redemption.

Assertions of biblical inerrancy are made in reference to the original autographs only. None of these is in existence, nor is there any reason to believe that we will ever have access to them.[2] We do not need them.

Paul Rees observes that God could have dropped the Bible ready-made from the skies in two thousand or more languages. He chose not to *drop* it, but to *develop* it over long periods of time with the help of many human agents. God *didn't* bestow it; He *built* it, piece by piece, event by event, writer by writer. It was initiated and interpenetrated by heaven, and cradled and colored by earth.[3]

The marvel of the Scriptures is not that they are the results of precise verbal dictation, but that they are the distillation of God's breath in written form through finite men; they are God-breathed, inspired, and form a reliable text for knowing God. Yes, God has spoken, but He has spoken to the spirits of mortal people like you and me.

Though breathed into and through imperfect human instruments, the Scriptures retain the integrity of God. More than sixty references state that the information in the Bible came from God's mouth. Yet, on their way to us the Scriptures came through the hearts, tongues, and pens of mortal men. He could have done it another way, but this was God's way. In this light, it was the best way.

Inerrancy is the way that many have chosen to say, "The Bible is completely reliable, authoritative, and authentic in its life-giving message to mankind." This view may have made the margins too small, which disallows others to come by another path to respect the Bible as the Word of God. Many have come to a complete respect for the Scriptures' authority without demanding the use of the word "inerrancy" to describe it. Neither Luther, Calvin, Warfield, nor Berkhouwer totally agreed on semantics, yet it would be difficult to find fault with their high views of Scripture.

It may be possible to reach the transcendent realm of which this book speaks without going through inerrancy, but it is unlikely. If this view seems extreme to anyone, is it not better to risk *overstatement* on the high position of inspiration than to take a lesser view and risk *understatement*?

If word usages alien to a particular point of view have offended anyone, please stay and read on. In position I am an inerrantist, but in disposition I stand with anyone who has a high view of the absolute authority of the Scriptures. Do not leave me on a technicality.

So far, readers may have concluded that I am fundamental, conservative, liberal, or a fanatic. Without equivocation I now have deeper respect, greater excitement, loftier expectations and more determined commitment to the Bible as the Word of God than I can ever remember in my lifetime. If suspicion of that arises in the pages to come, please turn back to this section and review the following sections on the Bible as a threefold miracle.

The Bible is what it is because of God's miraculous power in human history. Its own testimony is that it is inspired, God-breathed, and is profitable for doctrine, reproof, correction, and instruction in righteousness. (see 2 Tim. 3:16.)

The Scriptures are the result of three distinct phenomena, miracles by any standard. By their nature these miracles are residual, permanent, and tamperproof in time and eternity.

The Miracle of Inspiration

"Inspiration" is that influence of God's Spirit upon the minds of the Scripture writers, which made their writings a record of divine revelation. This is far beyond any use of "inspiration" as a reference to heightened human emotions or abilities. The Greek word is *theopneustos* and literally means "God-breathed." Thus, to believe in inspiration is to believe that the Scriptures are from the distillation of God's very breath as He spoke through human instruments and caused them to write what they heard. Repeated references to the breath of God are allusions to His speaking voice.

In Genesis He created the world, the cosmos, with the breath of His mouth. "And God said, 'Let there be light,' and there was light" (Gen. 1:3, NIV). The psalmist declares, "By the word of the LORD were the heavens made; their starry host by the breath of his mouth. For he spoke and it came to be; he commanded, and it stood firm" (Ps. 33:6,9, NIV).

Just as the breath of God brought all energy, matter, and life into being, His spoken words were formulated by men, upon whom He breathed, into a written document called Scripture.

The Miracle of Preservation

Inspiration without the miracle of preservation would be lost over time. "Preservation" is that influence of the Spirit of God upon the minds of Scripture translators and upon the texts themselves, which guarantee that the original message would arrive safe and sound in each generation. This divine preservation of Scripture is no less a miracle than the breath of God which originated it. And He continues to perpetuate it with its message intact to every age.

The devil could easily have distorted the original Scriptures or even stolen them in any era of time. Men could not live long enough to be guardians of Scriptures, nor have they ever had the power in themselves to counteract Satan's work. Without God's protection and power, it would have been a hopeless task to guard the Scriptures through various translations, cultures, and eras.

Praise the Lord for the benefit of the Holy Spirit's continuing ministry to protect, clarify, and keep pure the message of God once breathed upon the saints of old. The Word of God in the Scriptures is a miracle among us, and God is committed to its protection against all who would destroy it.

The Miracle of Illumination

The third miracle is as real as the first and the second. It is the miracle of illumination, the influence of the Spirit of God upon the minds of Scripture teachers and students, which causes their learning to transcend the realms of natural understanding. Plainly put, the same Holy Spirit who breathed it and presided over its preservation is now here to illumine it and make it alive. Unless and until a person has supernatural understanding of the Scriptures, he or she is left to mere mortal intellect to discern God's message. He who spoke it the first time, however, is present to illumine it and give us understanding beyond the borders of human intellect.

A tragedy of our day is the weak emphasis on this third and vital miracle. It is as if God miraculously spoke it, miraculously preserved it, and now has left the explanation and declaration of the Scripture to the best of human minds and methods. Not so! He has not ceased His work. He is neither mute nor motionless. He still speaks and will be heard by those who listen. He still works and will be seen by those who look. We may learn the backgrounds and the original languages and strictly obey all the rules of sound hermaneutics, but if we do not have the Spirit of God touching our understanding, we will be barren. If we listen to Him, we will hear; if we look to Him, we will see. Belief of this is required to move to that transcendent realm of power.

Three great miracles: the first, inspiration, has to do with the Bible's supernatural origination; the second, preservation, has to do with its supernatural continuation; and the third, illumination, has to do with its supernatural explanation.

The validity and credibility of the Bible rests not upon one of these alone, but upon all three. To dismiss one of them is to destroy the value of the other two.

Without preservation there is no guarantee that today's Bible is even similar to the original inspired autographs. No matter how flawless and perfect the original autographs, they are worthless without supernatural influence in preserving them. If we have inspiration and preservation but lack illumination, we are in deep trouble. Though the first two are of inestimable value, without illumination we are at sea without a rudder—left to interpret and understand the Scripture with the intellect and logic of unaided minds. History is littered with false and aberrant doctrines which resulted from private interpretations of the Scripture.

Opening upon the glorious landscape of the knowledge of God, Scripture's door swings on these three hinges, or miracles. The magnificent structure of written truth, our Bible has stood, stands, and will always stand with these three monumental and timeless miracles. If there is a higher view to be considered, I would subscribe to it. Having a high view of Scripture is crucial, but just as crucial is continued study and keeping those views under constant surveillance and reassessment. It seems wise to keep in mind that it is constantly and imminently possible to allow one's view of Scriptures to rise in importance above the value of the Scriptures themselves. I need to ask myself:

> ➤ Is my view of Scripture the result of blind presumption or a conviction that has resulted from careful prayer and study?
> ➤ Are the grounds of my view inherent in the present texts themselves?
> ➤ Have I maintained my view of Scripture with confident faith or thoughtless defensiveness?
> ➤ Is there room in the evangelical fold for views which might differ from mine in semantics? Do I begin to compromise when I even entertain dialogue regarding these views?
> ➤ Have I studied, to my satisfaction, the history of the battle for the Bible? Do I have an understanding of the vernacular which has surrounded these recurring controversies?
> ➤ Have I behaved in a manner becoming to Jesus Christ, or have I done what Charles Wesley suggested about those who were involved in the heated Arminian-Calvinistic debate on predestination: "Alas, they murdered love with truth"?

As an inerrantist, I am convicted that there are other questions that need to be addressed to the whole issue which has occupied the attention and energy of thousands of people over the decades.

Question 1

Why insist upon the use of the word "inerrancy"?

I am for using the best word or words, and obviously have used this one myself, but could I use another word and win the same ground for the case of biblical authority and truthfulness? Is there one that might be used in dialogue which is not as inflammatory as "inerrancy" seems to be?

If the high ground inerrantists are seeking to win is that of the complete reliability of the Scriptures, it is possible that by overuse of "inerrancy" we may have weakened our own position. By insisting that everyone use the word, we may have eroded whatever ground we had to discuss the issues.

It also seems that those who choose not to be involved in the front-line struggle are unfairly accused of being weak in their view of inspiration. Were we to use other words, such as *integrity, fidelity, infallibility, reliability, credibility,* or *authority* along with the word inerrancy, we might be approaching a more palatable view of its trustworthiness. If another word or phrase would bring us together for talk, let's use it.

Question 2

If inerrancy is said to refer to the original autographs only, and no one among us has seen them, are we claiming something that is unprovable?

Are we fair to insist on the perfection of the original autographs as a qualification for true evangelical orthodoxy? Why should perfection or lack of it add to or take from the present validity of Scripture? I was saved, called to preach, filled with the Spirit, and grew in Christ using the *King James Version* of the Scriptures. Some of the word usages are almost exactly opposite to modern usages. *Let* in our English means to "allow"; in King James English it meant to "disallow." *Prevent* in King James' day meant to "precede"; in our modern usage it means to "keep from or disallow."

I have never been confused or bothered by these breakdowns in language for one moment. If such imperfections are involved in modern translations and our faith is not crushed, why should our faith fade even if there were variances in the original autographs?

If God did not verbally dictate word for word the original autographs but sounded the message to and through the minds of flawed men, are we to be shocked faithless when there are variations of description between them? I think not! It is said that Origen knew that the New Testament was not written in the best Greek. But to him, that was unimportant because the revelation did not consist in the words but in the things revealed.

Question 3

Is it possible that in putting all our eggs in one basket of inerrancy we have imperiled the faith of many who have been of-

fended by our zealous insistence that the vehicle which brings us the Word of God be absolutely perfect?

Perhaps this "all-or-nothing-at-all" approach has caused some to say, "I cannot honestly agree with your idea of inerrancy; therefore, I cannot believe in the inspiration of Scripture at all!" A myriad of people in the world do not share my commitment to inerrancy but love Jesus as much as I, walk in integrity as I seek to do, and are as committed to the value and trustworthiness of the Scriptures as I. In our zeal to defend the Bible against those we suspected of being its detractors, we may have overreacted, making claims beyond propriety or engaging in warfare, when we might have engaged in prayer meetings followed by meaningful discussions.

Church history reveals some similar episodes. When Marcion and his followers rejected the Old Testament as an unworthy book with a false idea of God, Origen and others quickly reacted. They defended the seemingly harsh actions of God in the Old Testament by suggesting that each passage had several levels of truth: spiritual, moral, and eschatalogical. Overuse of this allegorical method of interpretation greatly complicated later understanding of certain passages of Scripture. Origen's motives were sterling; his methods were questionable.

In the seventeenth century the Socinians, based in Poland, launched attacks on some of the great doctrines of Scripture, including the Trinity and the resurrection. The Reformers, followers of Luther and Calvin, mounted counterattacks against them. They claimed that the Bible's full authority stood on the foundation that the vowel-points were inspired. It turned out that the vowel-points in the Old Testament text were not added until a thousand years after the Old Testament was completed.

A similar thing may well have happened again in our day. In reaction to alleged tendencies toward liberalism in their institutions, some Southern Baptists mounted a well-organized campaign to purge the denomination of all who did not hold to the inerrancy view of Scripture. The campaign, labeled a "holy war" by some, has been decisively won on the national scale by the conservatives. While I applaud the tenacity of the conservatives, I question the expenses of the battle in damaged relationships, divided churches, and even broken lives. Could we have achieved our goal in some better way? I believe we could. Might we now be in revival had we gone to the same expense to gather in prayer meetings across the continent to pray for God's mercy and grace upon us all? Not in many years has so much energy been expended by so many to win so little ground. We have now "won" that ground to some degree, but the battle is far from over. Now the battle lines are blurred, no institution is untouched, and all programs for global evangelism have been affected. Readers may not agree with me on the preceding pages, but I shall have my purpose fulfilled if they will only ask the questions I am suggesting and seek an answer in prayer that satisfies the soul.

Question 4

What other method might we use to bring the Bible to its highest recognition of credibility; or, put another way, what is the best way to prove to the world on the eve of the twenty-first century that the Bible is, in fact, the Word of God?

I'm glad I asked! For the answer to this all-important question, let us observe the sons of the Reformation. In their day the Roman Catholic Church declared that the Bible was of value because it (the church) said so—period! The church also insisted that common folk could not understand the Bible so they had best leave interpretation to the church and clergy. The Reformers came to realize that within the truths of the Bible were the seeds of its authentication. Among them was the Holy Spirit, who inspired the contents of Scripture! The Holy Spirit gives the Bible self-authenticating power as He moves upon the printed words to give them life.

Coming to grips with the power of the Word that spoke the worlds into existence, the Word that burned uncontainably in the hearts of the prophets, the Word that prompted faith in the Gentiles as Paul preached it, the Reformers realized that the ultimate proof of its authority lay in the power of the Holy Spirit who inspired its beginning.[4]

Rather than engage in arguments or plan a political revolution to win higher ground for the Bible, they preached it in the power of the Holy Spirit! Reverence for the Bible should lead to preaching it faithfully in the power of the One who produced its contents by inspiration.

If we conservatives have no more power than those who have liberalized the Scripture, what great advantage do we have? Why bother winning more points if the points we have won are lifeless? Dead orthodoxy is as useless as cold liberalism. If winning the point for inerrancy has not brought us to a fresh anointing which breaks the yoke of the bondages of our day, we are still short of what we need to touch our world.

We must have the power of the Word of God released through the lives of the adherents of Scripture. There is no substitute for the power of God. Neither dedicated scholarship, knowledge of the original languages, nor fanatic zeal will enthrone the Bible in its rightful place in the mind of modern man. Demonstrations of the power of God in Christian preachers and preaching will help show the world the Bible's unimpeachable credibility.

Carl F. H. Henry thoughtfully suggested, "A Bible unencumbered with theories and standing on its own invulnerable support may be far more powerful than the one propped up by the retaining walls engineered by resolute evangelicals."[5]

What proof did the prophets have that what they were hearing and speaking was in fact God's Word? Nothing but the power of the Word itself! What proof did the Thessalonians need that Paul was preaching the truth? Nothing but the power of the Holy Spirit speaking in power and demonstration.

> For our gospel came not unto you in word only,
> but also in power, and in the Holy Ghost,
> and in much assurance;
> as ye know what manner of men we were
> among you for your sake.
> —1 Thessalonians 1:5

> And my speech and my preaching
> was not with enticing words of man's wisdom,
> but in demonstration of the Spirit and of power.
> —1 Corinthians 2:4

Power such as Paul exercised, duplicated in twentieth-century teaching and preaching of the Scripture, is likely to win the higher ground with far greater efficiency than lingering debates and political manipulations.

After dealing with one lurking problem in the next chapter, we will turn to the high ground of the Word of God with power.

‹∙

The point at issue here
is not so much the fact that God has spoken but
whether or not God is still speaking. He has spoken.
All believers are convinced of that. But of late not all
are convinced that God still speaks. Since
communication is the central factor in a living
relationship, this is crucial.
To believe that God stopped speaking with the canon
of Scripture is to subvert Scripture, to make it less
than it is, and disallow intimacy with the living God.
—JRT

Chapter 2

The Hovering Heresy

Unlike other heresies that land and wreak havoc on the landscape, this one has hovered over every generation since the canon of Scripture was completed. It seldom possesses folks; it just floats in the theological atmosphere and continues to influence many.

I am not accusing anyone of this heresy. I do not think I have ever heard anyone actually articulate it. Nor have I met anyone who would argue for it. But I have a feeling that I may have lived much of my life in the shadow of this heresy and fear that much of Christendom is there still.

The hovering heresy is the notion that God used to be *articulate* and *active* and is now *mute* and *motionless*. It is the idea that since God gave us a Book, He does not need to communicate with His world anymore.

Does that sound far-fetched to you? Are you aware that much of the church today possesses a spiritual world view in line with this mentality?

You say, "I don't know anyone who would make such a claim." While that may be true, there are many believers today who live close to the edge of that heresy.

It seems to have emerged soon after the canon of Scripture was finished. Since the Bible is the Word of God, some reasoned, "God has had His say and that is that. What He has spoken is both perfect and complete. We have all the revelation we will ever need." And this silent supposition (that God has finished with speaking) floats around the church today largely unchallenged.

Recently I was talking to a friend who had just come from a prayer meeting in which, while praying, he had asked for a word from God about some direction in his life. He was accosted afterward by two preacher friends, one of whom said, "I really have a problem with the prayer you prayed. Don't you know that everything you need to know is found in the Bible and that God doesn't speak anymore?" My friend was still in shock. I repeat, I have never met anyone who has said to me, "God does not speak anymore," but I hear it every now and again in the atmosphere.

At least two mistaken notions feed this mentality which espouses a now-silent God. The first is that *if we have the highest view of Scripture we must conclude that what we have in the pages of the Bible is enough.* God does not need to speak because He has already spoken, and what He has spoken was breathed through men into a document we have designated as *The Book.* To declare that the Bible is all the Word of God is not to say that the Bible is a record containing all that God has ever said or is ever going to say. I have written several books. Frankly I would not feel pleased if someone were to say to me, "Jack, because I have read what you said, out of respect for your books I have resolved not to listen to anything you now have to say." That kind of honor I can do without!

The highest honor you and I can pay to the written Word of God is to believe what it says when it declares, "Man shall not live by bread alone, but by every word of God" (Luke 4:4). If this passage were not for us, surely Jesus would have suggested that this truth was timed to terminate with the close of the apostolic age or the finishing of the canon. He then would have another word for us, such as, "Man shall not live by bread alone but by every word written in the Scriptures."

The second factor in the mentality which silences God's voice in our generation may well be *the dangers involved in emphasizing that we can indeed hear Him.* There are murderers on death row right now who will declare to their dying breath, "God told me to do it." There are folks bouncing off the walls in churches across the country who are "hearing from God." There are preachers who are out to fleece the flock of God, saying, "God is telling me right this minute to tell you to send your money to me."

The proliferation of slick charlatans and wild-eyed fanatics does not do away with the glorious truth of a present-tense God who has not lost His voice. It would be less threatening, perhaps, to hold to the view of a silent heaven than to believe that at any given moment, in any given place, God could speak to any given person or group. A silent heaven can pose problems too, however. As A. W. Tozer expressed it:

> I believe that much of the religious unbelief is due to a wrong belief and wrong feeling for the Scriptures of Truth. A silent God suddenly began to speak in a book and when the book was finished lapsed into silence again forever. Now we read a book as the record of what God said when He was for a brief time in a speaking mood. With notions like that in our heads how can we believe?[6]

Every Christian on the planet should read chapter 6 in Tozer's book, *The Pursuit of God.* The chapter is entitled "The Speaking Voice." In it he says, "God is forever seeking to speak Himself out in creation. He is by His nature continuously articulate. He fills the world with His speaking voice. One of the great realities with which we have to deal is the voice of God in His world. The briefest and only satisfying cosmogony (how the world came into being) is this: 'He spake and it was done.' The why of natural law is the living voice of God imminent in His creation."[7]

Tozer continues,

> And this Word of God which brought all worlds into being cannot be understood to be the Bible, for it is not a written word at all, but the expression of the will of God spoken into the struc-

ture of all things. This Word of God is the breath of God filling the world with living potentiality. The voice of God is the most powerful force in nature, indeed the only force in nature, for all energy is here only because the power-filled Word is being spoken.[8]

There are safety measures we should use as we approach the conviction that God can and does speak today. Most of what He will say, He will say through the Scriptures. They come alive only when He enlivens them and speaks through them. When we receive impressions, messages, dreams, and visions that we believe are of God, we should turn immediately to the written Word of God to evaluate, confirm, or negate the message. It should be remembered in this process that the canon of Scripture is complete and will never require addition. Faithfulness to this fact, however, does not require that we silence the speaking voice of God now or in succeeding generations.

Thus we are wise to judge not only our interpretations of Scriptures in the light of other Scriptures, but all other impressions, visions, dreams, and revelations we believe to be of God. While we do not make law of the interpretations of the divines of the past, we do well to honor the work of those whose reputations for spirituality and scholarship have stood like a granite wall through the years.

Deism Revisited

The view of a silent God may have grown from an overreaction to the extreme supernaturalism which was prevalent in Europe before the Reformation. The emphasis on supernaturalism without the power of God filtered down to dangerous superstition. Against these abuses Luther revolted. Unfortunately the revolt didn't stop with Luther but continued to broaden into one against any institutional religion. The result was an atmosphere of intense anti-supernaturalism. By the end of the eighteenth century, the effects of what came to be called "the Enlightenment" were felt across the continent of Europe. Immanuel Kant, an Enlightenment philosopher, wrote an article in 1784 in which he declared,

The Enlightenment was man's coming to age. It was man's emergence from the immaturity which caused him to rely on such external authorities as the Bible, the Church, and the state to tell him what to think and do. No generation should be bound by creeds and customs of bygone ages. To be so bound is an offense against human nature, whose destiny lies in progress.

Kant, Newton, Rousseau, Voltaire, and American founders Benjamin Franklin and Thomas Jefferson were Enlightenment thinkers. They acknowledged the existence of God but held what was commonly called the "deistic" view, namely, that God was the Creator but had left humans in charge of the issues of conduct and reason. As time went along, human beings became more and more impressed with their intelligence and less and less God-conscious. The pendulum swung from supernaturalism and superstition to rationalism and materialism. Science began to be viewed as the savior that would release humankind from enslavement to the social, political, and religious bondages of that day.

The Age of Reason had dawned and the Enlightenment thinkers were, in the words of one observer:

> Highly critical of the traditional appeal, made by Christian apologists, to fulfilled prophecy and miracles as proofs of the divine attentuation of Christianity. They argued that the Old Testament passages that were alleged to be fulfilled did not really predict the events concerned and that the New Testament miracles did not really happen.

Our Western world-view is greatly influenced by the Enlightenment mentality. There is a tendency toward a sort of neo-deism or the warmed-over Enlightenment approach to reality. Our educational processes lean toward the Aristotelian approach to learning, which majors on the senses and reason without current revelation.

Biblicism

If it is heretical to strip the Scriptures of their divine nature, as the rationalists did, it is also heretical to so exalt the Scriptures as a document that we revere them more than the living God in our midst. To twist the Scriptures in such a manner as to strip God of His right to speak to us through them, as well as apart from them, may be a more subtle heresy than those the Enlightenment spawned. If the Scripture needs to be rescued from the rational mentality in liberalism, it may also need to be rescued from the hands of its defenders who would traffic in its truth to seek methodically to destroy all opposition. It is a sobering realization that the Bible may suffer as much in the hands of its defenders as in the hands of its detractors.

In summary, let us declare that we believe the Bible to be the Word of God, reliable in all its parts, and able to make us wise unto salvation. Let us gladly confirm, in addition, that the God of the Bible still lives to speak through its pages, making clear what He said to the ancients. Let us be done with anything that smacks of Enlightenment theology and ask the Holy Spirit, who is no less than the on-site, present tense, here-and-now, contemporary God, to breathe on us anew.

Let us allow the breath of God to blow away the "hovering heresy" that God is no longer speaking and hear Him as He speaks to us and our age. God did not leave His Word to be read at a distance by unaided minds. He spoke a Book and lives in His spoken words, constantly speaking His words and causing the power of them to persist across the years.[9]

Let us forever put to rest the myth of a silent God and allow His Spirit to do His work. When Jesus was seeking to prepare His followers for a coming era when He would no longer be with them in the flesh, He spoke of another Comforter. This Comforter, obviously a Person and not just a mere influence, was to do several things, all of which involved communication. Most of this teaching takes place in John, chapters 14 and 16:

[He] will teach you all things
and will remind you of everything that I have said to you.
—John 14:26, NIV

When he is come, he will reprove the world of sin,
and of righteousness, and of judgment.
—John 16:8

But when he, the Spirit of truth, comes,
he will guide you into all truth. He will not speak on his own;
he will speak only what he hears,
and he will tell you what is yet to come.
—John 16:13

[The Spirit] shall take of mine, and shall shew it unto you.
—John 16:15

Every one of these tasks require communication, disclosure, revelation, and interaction. Of course, the Holy Spirit will use the written Scripture, but He is not bound to its pages in the issue of making His will known to us.

It is no more unusual to expect that there are words that God has to say to us today than it was when He walked among us in the visible Person of Christ. To seek to silence Him now is the height of inconsistency. The Bible stands to enhance the communication between heaven and earth, not to terminate it. Yes, I can hear God in the Book, and that Book is the proper judge of the authenticity or the fallibility of subsequent words heard in our midst. His later speakings will never be out of accord with His former speaking. In this is our safety.

May we wash our minds of any fallout from the rationalism of the past or present. May we move out from under the cloud that has hovered over the church for centuries. God has spoken, and He speaks still. This we must believe if we are to experience the Word of God with power.

ஃ

The Word of God
was spoken before it was written.
Jesus was seen and touched and heard
before He was written about.
It is this spokenness,
the living, dynamic creativity, that characterizes
the Word of God above everything else.
—Eugene Peterson

Chapter 3
_____

What Is the Word of God?

For nearly three years preceding this writing, I have been immersed in studying and preaching on little else but the Word of God. It has consumed every area of my mind. I go to sleep thinking about it. I wake up with it on my mind. I dream about it and am occupied with it during the daytime. The answer to the question posed in the title of this chapter has comprised a vital part of these months of consideration. In order for you to understand how I arrived where I am, it will be necessary to tell you about the journey.

It began with a phone call from a friend who, three weeks before, had spent the night as our house guest. He quietly informed me that cancer had been discovered in his body and that he and his wife were studying options as to what procedures to take. I was shocked and somewhat angry, not at God or any person, but with the whole picture. My father was taken some years ago by cancer, so I suppose I have a justifiable grudge against this insidious disease.

In the same time frame (perhaps the same day), another telephone call revealed that another friend of many years was diagnosed as having pancreatic cancer. My anger increased into smoldering rage. *It isn't fair*, I thought. *No power should be great enough to interrupt the lives of the children of God or to threaten their ministries.*

My anger soon turned to prayer. I was determined to get some answers from the Lord on these two situations. As I prayed, the Lord turned my mind to a study I had done some twenty years before on the subject of the power of words and the power of the Word of God. I was catapulted into a fresh examination of the claims of the Bible for the Word of God.

Almost immediately as I prayed for these two friends, a passage for each of them came to mind. In the first case it was John 11:4, in which Jesus replied to the news that his friend, Lazarus, was sick. He said, "This sickness is not unto death, but for the glory of God, that the Son of God might be glorified thereby." As I prayed for my other sick friend, the Lord brought another verse to mind in Psalm 139:16. It says, "All the days ordained for me were written in your book before one of them came to be" (*New English Bible*). *The Living Bible* says it like this, "You saw me before I was born and scheduled every day of my life before I began to breathe. Every day was recorded in your book."

I shared these words with both of these men. Of course, I was not the only one to get words for them, and the words I received were not the only ones which were confirmed. But for these months a watching world has witnessed the power of the Word of God in both of their lives, not only to extend life, but to enhance the quality of life by bringing them into sharper focus.

These men are well known in the Christian world. Both are authors and positioned in strategic places of influence in the world. The first is Jamie Buckingham. After being informed that he had weeks to live, he and his wife, Jackie, simply took refuge in the Word of God. The result was that over eighteen months of quality life and ministry were granted to Jamie. That story is beautifully chronicled in his book *Summer of Miracles.*

The second is Jim Mahoney. I have debated mentioning their names, lest they, and not the Word of God, become the center of attention. Neither they nor I would have it so. I have shared these events so that you might know the point of departure on this study.

I could mention many others—some with whom I have prayed, others for whom I have prayed. I have seen some astounding cases of healing while others have died. I have not, in this time frame, been in a meeting where people have not been healed, though this has not been the thrust of the meetings. I have found that when people come alive to the concept of the power of the Word of God and begin to speak it in faith something happens. In the cases of Jamie and Jackie Buckingham and Jim and Shannon Mahoney, the Word of God in their hearts and on their lips became their very life-source. Though both Jim Mahoney and Jamie Buckingham are now in heaven, their testimonies of the power of the Word of God ring fresh in the hearing of those who knew them both.

As I saw the effect of the Word of God on their bodies and minds, I was brought to a re-examination of my view of the overall concept of the Word of God. I remembered with pleasure the previous joy of discovering and preaching on the power of the Word of God and the accompanying power that comes through sharing it in confession. Never before, however, had I entertained the magnitude of the power that I was now seeing the Word of God to have, not only in these men but in my own life as well. Both of them, through trusting in the power of God's Word, won years of meaningful life and walked unhurried into the presence of God. Their homegoings during the preparation of this volume do not take away a particle of the credibility of the power of the Word of God from my mind.

I feel that there is a higher position on biblical authority than just believing the Bible to be accurate and reliable. If we believe that all the claims of Scripture are credible, then we will believe its inherent testimony about the power of the Word of God. If we are to understand to any degree the power of the Word of God, we must know what we are talking about when we use the term, "the Word of God." In order to do this we must know what the Bible is talking about when it uses the term.

So I ask you, "To what (or whom) does the Bible refer when it uses the term, the Word of God?" This is not as easily answered as we first might think. Our rapid response would normally be, "Well, the Bible, of course!" Yes, the Bible is the Word of God, but the Bible is not necessarily referring to the Bible when it mentions the Word of God. That would be quite impossible, since the Bible, as we have it, was not around at the time such references were made. In fact, when the part of the Bible that was around during those writings was referenced, it was called "Scripture" or "the Scriptures." No reference in the Bible to the Word of God, as far as I have been able to observe, is a clear reference to a document or something written.

Now, you have not heard me say that the Bible is not the Word of God. I believe that it *is* the Word of God beyond any shadow of a doubt. But no reference in the Bible to the Word of God is a reference to itself per se. Thus, we must conclude that the references to the Word of God are references to far more than a written and published document.

For effect, here are some Scriptures that reference the Word of God, substituting the words "written document" for the word or words appearing in the Bible.

> By the *written document* were the heavens made.
> —Psalm 33:6

> Is not my *written document* like as a fire? saith the Lord;
> and like a hammer that breaketh the rock in pieces?
> —Jeremiah 23:29

> So shall my *written document* be that goeth forth out of my
> mouth; it *(the written document)* shall not return unto me void,
> but it shall accomplish that which I please, and it shall prosper
> in the thing whereto I sent it.
> —Isaiah 55:11

> Through faith we understand that the worlds were framed by
> *the written document,* so that the things which are seen were not
> made of things which do appear.
> —Hebrews 11:3

> The *written document* is quick (alive), and powerful,
> and sharper than any two edged sword,
> piercing even to the dividing asunder of soul and spirit,
> and of the joints and marrow, and is a discerner of the
> thoughts and intents of the heart.
> —Hebrews 4:12

It is patently obvious that these references are not to a document but to something far broader. This does not cheapen the Scriptures but places them in proper perspective, where their full purpose can be realized. As I began to walk down this path of study, I feared a loss of reverence for the Bible as a Book. The exact opposite is occurring. The more power I see exercised in the spiritual realm the more respect and awe I have for this glorious document.

The Word of God, as the Bible speaks of it, predates the Scriptures as eternity predates time; it is greater than but includes time. In its fullest significance, the Word of God as we are referring to it is greater than but includes the Bible.

The Word of God was around before what the prophets said became the written Word of God. The Word of God was in action before what Paul wrote became the Word of God in our Bible. This is a necessary concept if we are to know the power of God's Word.

Power is the capacity to generate change. If we equate the references in the Bible to the Word of God as a document, we have confined ourselves to expectations of what a document, albeit the Bible, can do. A book, even the glorious Bible, can only do what a book can do. A book does not have life. We are informed that faith comes by hearing and hearing by the Word of God (Rom. 10:17). You cannot hear a book; you can only read it. Faith does not come by reading; faith comes by hearing! For hearing to occur there must be a voice. Without something said there is no hearing.

I have pondered for years the question, "Is the Bible the Word of God?" Many in our world would answer in the negative. Some of them might hedge and say, "Well, I believe that it *contains* the Word of God." For myself, I repeat, the Bible is the Word of God, period! But I want you to examine the following statement carefully and consider it critically:

The Bible is the Word of God (as it refers to the Word of God) only when the Holy Spirit who inspired it enlivens it. Only then does it have life and power. Until then it is document; document is letter, and letter kills. This is the reason why in the Western world, where so much Bible is preached, there is so much spiritual death. Emphatically, this condition is not the Bible's fault but the failure of humankind to depend upon the Holy Spirit.

At first reading the above statement seems to border on heresy. Read it again, because what is being said here is vital to the remainder of this book. It may appear that I am seeking to downgrade the Bible; that is the farthest thing from my intention. I am seeking to arrive at the highest position for the Word of God as the Bible refers to it. In doing so you and I will succeed in bringing the Bible itself to its highest position and thus, its highest potential.

The many references to the Word of God in the Bible could not refer to the Bible as such because claims are made that no book can accomplish, not even the greatest book in the world. No book is alive or full of energy. No book existed prior to the creation of the world. No book, as a printed document, will survive. The Word of God as truth will survive time and will be vital in eternity. As a document the Scriptures may or may not be preserved and put on display in heaven. The Bible has never claimed for itself eternal status as a document. No book can accomplish a spiritual birth in which a sinner is suddenly converted, delivered from the powers of darkness, and translated into the kingdom of Christ. No book, at least of any size, can abide inside me. Yet I am implored to let the Word dwell in me richly (Col. 3:16).

There are references to the Word of God used in the same passage with the references to Scripture, which emphasizes this all-important point. In John 5:38-39, Jesus says, "And ye have not his word abiding in you: for whom he hath sent, him ye believe not. Search the scriptures; for in them ye think ye have eternal life: and they are they which testify of me."

Jesus spoke these words to folks who were well-versed in the Scriptures, yet they were trying to kill Him because He had worked a miracle on the Sabbath day (John 5:16). They did not have the Word of God in them; yet their business called for the searching of the Scriptures daily.

When we speak of the Word of God in its highest expression, we are speaking of something distinct from a written document but inclusive of all that is recorded in that document (the Bible). The heart is distinct among the members of the body, but it is thankfully included as a part of the body. It is indispensably important to the body and yet cannot exist as a living entity apart from the body. So the written Word, the Scripture, is *distinct from but included in* the larger expression of the Word of God. It is in its functions the basis of the continued life of the body of Christ. The Scripture is the result of the breath of God, and when it is breathed upon again it is energized and animated to accomplish the will of God on earth.

In Acts 17, when Paul was preaching in Berea, the Bereans are recorded as doing a remarkable thing. They are described as being "more noble than those in Thessalonica, in that they received the word with all readiness of mind, and searched the scriptures daily, whether those things were so" (v. 11). They heard the Word of God from Paul, and they searched the Scriptures to confirm what he had said to be indeed the Word of God!

It is interesting to note that Jesus also said to the Pharisees, "For laying aside the commandment of God, ye hold the tradition of men, . . . making the word of God of none effect through your tradition" (Mark 7:8,13). Their tradition was based upon written Scripture. That Scripture was the result of the breath of God but had long since been exercised and interpreted by human minds without the breath of God upon it. Thus even the Scriptures had no life in them. The Pharisees had long since left the Word of God (in the larger expression) and had adopted traditions (letter of Scripture) which, in effect, had nullified the Word of God.

To acknowledge that Scripture and the Word of God are not identical references is not to depreciate the Scripture but to exalt the Word of God! As I have read and reread this section, I have been uncomfortable at times when sentences seem to suggest that the Word of God should be perceived as something different from the Bible. If that bothers you, it should! It is a crucial issue. The two can be different but they should not be. They were not meant to be. Any difference is imposed by us and not by the Word.

In the sensitive material to follow, we will see that, while the Word of God involves at least four vital and distinct considerations, *it is one!* In the end we will see that there is a corporateness to the Word of God. Damage always results when this corporateness is lost in our minds. The Word of God is not one of the following; it is all four! When we are through and God has done what I have prayed He would do, you will have a deeper respect and a loftier view of these facets of the Word of God than ever.

And yes, the Holy Scripture will mean more to you when we are through than it ever has. So stay with me!

ஃ

Before the Word of God was a document—
before it was anything—
it was a Person.
Though now a document, the Bible,
it is still a Person and always will be.
That is eternally changeless!

—JRT

Chapter 4

Exploring the Identity of the Word of God
The Word of God Is a Person

Before it was anything else, the Word was an invisible, eternal Person, co-existent, and co-equal in the Trinity. He eternally existed before the beginning. The Word has never been less than such a Person! Listen to John's lofty description of the Word (1:1-5):

In the beginning was the Word,
and the Word was with God, and the Word was God.
The same was in the beginning with God.
All things were made by him;
and without him was not any thing made that was made.
In him was life; and the life was the light of men.
And the light shineth in darkness;
and the darkness comprehended it not.

33

In this description of grandeur, we have the highest statement of the essential identity of the Word of God. We must never in our considerations of the Word of God leave out this factor. Jesus Christ is the Word of God! He has always been the Word of God. John's introduction is retrospective. "In the beginning was the Word"! When we are dealing with the Word of God, we are dealing with Someone eternal. In these early words of his gospel, John is giving us the first fact as to the identity of the Word of God. Before there was a sounded word, there was the Person of the Word. Before there was a written word, He was the Word. Long before Moses wrote a word or the prophets thundered out their word, He was the Word of God. Before Abraham was, He was. Before anything was, He was. Before He was (as a baby in Bethlehem), He was (as the eternal preincarnate Son of God).

Here is the grandest fact of human history:

> The Word was made flesh, and dwelt among us,
> (and we beheld His glory,
> the glory as of the only begotten of the Father,)
> full of grace and truth.
> —John 1:14

The Word of God, who was eternal, invisible, the Creator of heaven and earth, now becomes a human being, a baby human being! Here is the incarnation, an event which defies human understanding. He is named what He has always been in eternity, *the Word*. He is called what He was, the message from God. He is what God has said and what God has to say.

It was through the message from Gabriel that the Word of God was delivered to Mary. As that Word was spoken it was a seed inherent with the life of God (the Greek word for "seed" is *spermos* from which we get our word *sperm*). When she responded by receiving the Word, she was instantaneously impregnated by the Holy Spirit. When He was born the event is described in these terms: "The Word became flesh!"

It would be difficult to imagine that He would be brought up in any other manner than was afforded all Jewish boys—in the Scriptures. His ministry was a Word ministry. He cast out demons with the Word. He healed with the Word. He spoke the Word of God with authority. "And they were astonished at his doctrine: for his word was with power" (Luke 4:32).

So the Word was at first an eternal, invisible Person; then, in the fulness of time, He became flesh. Mystery of mysteries. Eternity puts on, for a while, the garments of time. God houses Himself in human flesh. He becomes His own Word incarnate in this world. He was, in fact, the embodiment of the Father's thought and being. Andrew Murray calls Him the "Speaking Self" of the Father.

Again, let it be said that here, and here alone, is the highest definition of the Word of God. The Word is a Person and that Person is Jesus, the Christ. He made that claim for Himself repeatedly. It was made for Him throughout the New Testament. In one of the last descriptions in Scripture of Him, He is called the Word of God. (See Rev. 19:13.)

Hebrews, chapter 1, records that God has spoken through the prophets in many different times and many different ways but in the last days has spoken unto us by His Son. Never should we seek to understand the phrase "the Word of God" apart from Christology, who He is, what He has said and is saying. Our view of the written Word will never rise above our view of the Person of the Word, Jesus Christ.

The Word of God Is a Dynamic Declaration

The Word of God is not only a Person, but it is *what God says*. And when He speaks it is always with power. Seven times in the first chapter of Genesis, we have the record, "And God said" (Gen. 1:3,6,9,14,20,24,26). The Word was God's chosen means by which everything created was brought into being. This is a vital and unavoidable scientific fact. The sooner science admits this, the sooner the puzzles of the universe will be understood. Listen to the words of scientist W. J. Bauer:

> God, an infinite person of infinite power and existence in and outside time, has created by means of His Word and through words. We can see evidence of this in every living organism, be it plant or animal. Every living cell has a DNA system which is the "sine quo non" of its biological life. Life exists only where the "word system" called the DNA is present.
>
> The DNA directs the building of living cells using non-living materials such as water, calcium, nitrogen, iron, carbon, hydrogen, etc. The DNA is purely and simply an information system. Meaning in such systems is a function of the sequence of the ele-

ments of communication, as the letters and words in a book, and the nucleotides in the DNA chains.

Scientists today are trying to "read" the entire DNA in humans. It will take many years, perhaps decades (even with the invention of "speed-reading" devices) to read the entire thing.

There is no more direct evidence that the method of creation was the spoken Word of God. Not only do we see it in the DNA information system, but we have the record in Scripture that God "breathed into his nostrils the breath of life, and Adam became a living soul." This is a very direct statement which is evidenced from the DNA information system which each person has inherited from his ancestors.

I am enthusiastic about the power of the Word of God! That Word and that Word alone is all that lives in the world in which we find ourselves. *That Word is the sole source of our biological life,* [emphases mine] as the DNA, given to our ancestor, Adam, when God breathed into his nostrils the breath of life, is the only component in our physical bodies which can command dead materials like water to build themselves into living cells. And it is the same language for all living creatures, both plant and animal, because it came from the spoken Word of the same living God. One of the obvious principles which can be observed in nature is all life comes from life. We do not observe life coming from dead things. The only scientific fact is that life comes from life. This is all that has been observed. It is called the Law of Biogenesis.[10]

I hope you read that statement carefully. If not, read it again. A man of science is saying that the only source of everything—life, matter, and energy, and time—is none other than the Word of God! It is significant in this study and in our lives that we understand this basic fact of life in the universe, namely, that God's spoken word is the means by which everything was created. Dr. Bauer further says,

The fact is that only life begets life. This is true of the human spirit. It is dead, apart from its being responsive to the words of the God who is alive. That God is best understood in the form of the God-man, Jesus Christ. I invite everyone to recognize that Living God as the only source of true life, life with an eternal dimension to it, even for life in this present world in which we find ourselves. Come to the Source of living water and experience the joy, the peace, the love, the power, the sound mind, and all the other gifts which this living God is offering to each person who will trust what He is saying in His Word, the Bible.[11]

Some invitation for a scientist! The Word of God was a declaration of such power that it birthed the universe and all that is in it. From the Word of God are all energy, matter, and life derived. But keep in mind that the sound of His Word cannot be separated from the identity of His being.

The sound of His voice that was the agent of creation is inclusive of the Person of Christ. The voice and the Person are inseparable. He existed before the voice sounded in Genesis 1, and when the voice sounded He was the creative Word. They cannot be separated, but for some understanding it helps to distinguish them from each other.

We cannot leave this consideration without going on to say that at this present moment, the whole universe is being held together by the spoken Word of God. He "upholds all things by the word of his power" (Heb. 1:3).

The dynamic declaration, the Word of God, has pervaded the stretches of the universe and holds it together to accomplish God's purpose. God has said, "So shall my word be that goeth forth out of my mouth: it shall not return unto me void, but it shall accomplish that which I please, and, shall prosper in the thing whereto I sent it" (Isa. 55:11). This glorious matter of which we speak, the Word of God, has created the world, holds it together, and is vitally resident in the universe to bring it to its divine end.

As we have discussed its identity we have also observed the reason for its power. The Word of God is the very breath, the life of God. "By the word of the LORD were the heavens made; and all the host of them by the breath of his mouth. He spake, and it was done; he commanded, and it stood fast" (Ps. 33:6,9). The very breath of God gave the universe existence and remains to give life in the universe to all who receive His Word.

Here is an illustration that will give an idea how great the power of the Word of God really is:

In November of 1990 astronomers, through the use of a gigantic telescope, made a startling discovery. They found a concentration of stars that stretches for more than six million light years, more than sixty times larger than the Milky Way. It is the largest cluster of galaxies ever discovered. The new discovery was called Abell 2029 and is comprised of about one hundred trillion stars. The Milky Way, which includes the sun and its solar system, has about three billion stars. Abell 2029 is about a billion light years away and includes about a thousand galaxies, each with a billion stars. A light year is the distance light can travel in a year in a vacuum, about 186,000 miles per second. So a light year is approximately 5.89 trillion miles, give or take a few billion. Multiply one billion times 5.89 trillion and you have the number of miles between this galaxy and earth. That amounts to a figure of 5.89 followed by twenty-one zeroes! So this newly discovered cluster of galaxies, made up of a hundred thousand billion stars, is a trillion billion miles away! Does that stretch your mind? And to think that the Word of God gave birth to this and all other galaxies! It is the Word by which God holds all these galaxies together as well!

"Through faith we understand that the worlds were framed by the word of God" (Heb. 11:3). Of this declaration A. W. Tozer said,

> Again we must remember that God is referring here not to His written Word, but to His speaking voice. His world-filling voice, that voice which antedates the Bible by uncounted centuries, that voice which has not been silent since the dawn of creation, but is sounding still throughout the full far reaches of the universe.[12]

I am told that science generally holds to the idea that the universe is actually expanding at the speed of light. And the Word of God brought it all into existence and holds it together. That same Word has been and is being spoken over all creation and is being heard throughout all the galaxies in the vast universe, guaranteeing that the total will of God will be accomplished (Isa. 55:10-11)!

"Let them praise the name of the LORD: for he commanded, and they were created. He hath also stablished them for ever and ever: he hath made a decree which shall not pass" (Ps. 148:5-6).

"For this they willingly were ignorant of, that *by the word of God* the heavens were of old, and the earth standing out of the water and in the water: Whereby the world that then was, being overflowed with water, perished: But the heavens and the earth, which are now, *by the same word* are kept in store, reserved unto fire against the day of judgment and perdition of ungodly men" (2 Pet. 3:5-7, emphases added).

Again, whatever primary expression of the Word of God we are dealing with, we cannot, must not, leave out the others. The Word as a dynamic declaration cannot be separated from the Word as a Person, the eternal Christ. In reality it is He who was *in* the beginning and *from* the beginning and by whom all things are made. It is He who holds all things together. Listen to this lofty description of Him who is the Word:

"Who is the image of the invisible God, the firstborn of every creature: for by him were all things created, that are in heaven, and that are in earth, visible and invisible, whether they be thrones, or dominions, or principalities, or powers: all things were created by him, and for him: and he is before all things, and by him all things consist" (Col. 1:15-17).

When we speak of the Word holding the universe in place, we are speaking of a dynamic declaration still being sounded throughout the universe in concert with the glorious identity of the Son of God, the Lord Jesus Christ. We must never separate them! The whole created universe must be alive at this very moment with the triumphant expression, "Jesus Christ is Lord!"

The Word of God Is a Document

Throughout history God has caused a part of what He has purposed to say to be written in documents, beginning with the Books of Moses. This continued through the days of the apostles until in the second century documents were being circulated through the churches. In the fourth century they became recognized as the official canon of our Scripture, the Bible.

Just as the visible, physical Jesus was a distillation of what God had to say in a human body, the published Book, the Bible, is the distillation of the message of God in printed form. What a Book! Long before they were put together in their present form, the words had great potential power.

When read (as the Law) in times of dreadful decadence, the moral life of the nations was changed by the power of the sounded Word. In the days of Nehemiah, Ezra read the Law to the gathered people, and the result was that their consciences were smitten and the whole crowd wept (Neh. 8).

In Josiah's day the neglected book of the Law was brought before the people and read again. The result was a mighty spiritual revolution (2 Kings 22). The Spirit of God who breathed its contents enlivened it to revive the soul of the devastated nation.

Though the Word of God is a document in its narrowest definition, it is the glorious gift of God to humankind. It has survived the edicts of tyrants who sought to have it abolished forever. Its contents are the words of God, the words of His Christ, and the words of men whose words were made the Word of God by the power of the Spirit.

It has arrived in our day with the message that God originally intended intact. Its message is true. It has been the center of theological controversy in virtually every age of history. The devil hates it and would hide it and hush its holy voice. The intensity of the attacks from without have been equaled by the attacks from within, many times in the name of scholarship.

When God speaks today, it is generally through this holy Book. When God speaks to us of things not in the Scripture, it becomes a guide and a guard to evaluate what we hear and to protect us against shipwreck. God called me to salvation, but He used the Bible to bring me into it. He called me to preach, but it was within the context of being taught the printed Word of God, the Bible, that I responded to that call.

It should be remembered, that when the canon comprising the document which now makes up our Bible was finished, the Word of God did not cease being a Person. Nor did it cease being dynamic declaration. We now have a three-fold identity for the Word of God: *the Person,* at first, invisible and then becoming flesh and dwelling among us; then, a dynamic declaration that birthed all things; and *the document,* reliable, integrated, and true in every part.

These are interrelated and inseparable. We are the beneficiaries of their riches. To separate them is to dilute their meaning. When the Word as a Person became the sounded Word that created all matter, energy, and life, He did not cease to be who He was as the eternal Co-equal of God the Father and God the Holy Spirit. When the documents, written through the lives of mortal men, but breathed upon by the Spirit (breath) of God, became the Scripture, the Word did not cease to be a Person or a creative and sustaining Dynamic.

In the fourth century, when the canon of Scripture was officially recognized, a document, the Holy Bible, formally came to be recognized as the Word of God. If we may perceive a difference between the written Word and the Word made flesh, it is not in *essence* but in *expression*. The Scripture is to Jesus, the eternal Word, what a picture is to a person, what a musical score is to a symphony, and what a menu is to the meal of which it speaks.

But there is more! A fourth expression is worthy of our full consideration.

The Word of God Is a Life Source

It is the present tense living Word in our world which can be spoken, confessed, and released in power. Jesus modeled it when he spoke to diseases, demons, winds, and trees. It is the God-in-us Word that has brought about our spiritual birth and abides in us for the living of the life of Christ. "Being born again, not of corruptible seed, but of incorruptible, by the word of God, which liveth and abideth for ever" (1 Pet. 1:23).

It corresponds to the Person of the Word, the Lord Jesus Christ; is an extension of the dynamic declaration that brought the worlds into existence; and it is closely related to the infallible written Word, the Bible.

It is called the "Word of faith" in Romans 10:8-10.

> But what saith it? The word is nigh thee,
> even in thy mouth, and in thy heart:
> that is, the word of faith, which we preach;
> that if thou shalt confess with thy mouth the Lord Jesus,
> and shalt believe in thine heart
> that God hath raised him from the dead, thou shalt be saved.
> For with the heart man believeth unto righteousness;
> and with the mouth confession is made unto salvation.

This Word of God is the means of our birth in the Spirit and the power that resides in us in the Person of Jesus, the Word. It is in Him, yet it is not He. It is an extension of the dynamic that spoke the worlds into being, yet it is distinctly ours today. It is in accord with the written Word of God, the Bible, yet is distinct from the Bible as a document (distinct from but included). It may be a quote from the written Word, but it is alive by the Spirit and is more than reading or quoting from a document. The Bible is a record of God's speaking voice. This powerful entity, the present-tense Word of God, is a repeating of God's speaking voice. It is the believer saying what he hears.

This was modeled in Jesus when He confessed, "As I hear, I judge: and my judgment is just; because I seek not mine own will, but the will of the Father which hath sent me. If I bear witness of myself, my witness is not true" (John 5:30-31). Jesus was saying that He listened to what the Father said and repeated it. Thus what He said was always right. Prior to that He declared that He watched what the Father was doing and did it with Him. (See John 5:19.) If we could be as "in tune" with Him as He lives within us as He was with the Father, we could live more like He lived.

There are many strange things going on in the name of this wonderful Word in our midst. Only the Bible will keep us safe in these times. Being an infallible record of the speaking voice of God, the Bible forms an accurate grid by which we may determine, evaluate, and implement His present speaking voice. While the potential for danger is great in emphasizing that we can hear from God, it is just as dangerous to contain the "speaking" of God in a document. Admittedly, it would be more antiseptic to stay with the revelations of the past and not allow for any more illumined words from God. But the book is simply a document, albeit unerringly accurate, without the present expression of God.

God has spoken; to acknowledge that is basic. God is still speaking; to deny that is tragic. God is consistent, which means that He never violates former revelation with subsequent revelation. Because He is consistent we need not fear regarding His ability to remain consistent and to handle fraudulent contentions against the authority of His Word.

The present tense Word of God, alive in us, is vital and powerful on our lips and in our lives. Jesus spoke to a fig tree and cursed it by saying, "No man eat fruit of thee hereafter for ever" (Mark 11:14). When He and the disciples passed by later, they saw the tree was dead, withered from the roots up. When Peter called it to His attention, Jesus said, "Have faith in God [literally, "have the faith of God"]. For verily I say unto you, That whosoever shall say unto this mountain, Be thou removed, and be thou cast into the sea; and shall not doubt in his heart, but shall believe that those things which he saith shall come to pass; he shall have whatsoever he saith" (Mark 11:22-23). He was, in effect, saying, "What you have seen me do is within your capacities."

Now, immediately folks begin to "name it and claim it," "say it and get it," "blab it and grab it." Because of these extremes, others veer to the opposite side of the road toward the other ditch. While that other ditch (where we are confessing and claiming nothing) is safer, it is a ditch nonetheless. In avoiding one ditch we may have fallen into another just as perilous.

There are at least three things that need to be said in this regard as we move into the dimension of *the Word of God with power.*

First, while there is the potential for problems here, neglecting this great truth may prove of greater expense than the problems. So do not vacate the premises when words begin to fly from the spiritual realm. This is where the Bible will serve as our Protector and Guide, through the Holy Spirit. Those sounding this message, in the main, are men and women of God and need to be heard. Most of the time frauds are easy to spot. Many times their disciples have carried their teachings to such extremes that it is not recognizable as scriptural. New traditions develop around these mutations and all kinds of spiritual weirdness result.

In the second place, we have no right to expect that we will get what we say unless what we say is a result of what He has said to us. There are folks who are convinced that in them is the power to speak and to receive whatever they say. Some are getting what they say by bamboozling people into giving them what they say they have heard. Others are confessing things and are going away disappointed and disenchanted.

The Scripture in Mark 11 is clear, "Whosoever shall say unto this mountain, Be thou removed and be thou cast into the sea; and shall not doubt in his heart, but shall believe that those things which he saith will come to pass; he shall have whatsoever he saith." Remember that this was the word of Jesus, giving them authority to do it. We cannot go around indiscriminately saying to any "mountains" in our path, "Be moved!" If we do, we will be disappointed. However, if you get a word from God about that "mountain," whatever it is, start talking to the mountain! But be sure that it is *His* Word, not *yours.* If God has not said it, what we say has no power or promise!

Jesus said, "If I bear witness of myself, my witness is not true" (John 5:30). I cannot, in fact, take a word chosen from the Bible and expect that it will become reality until God has enlivened it as His present Word for me. Once He has, I can speak that Word and expect to receive the answer in the fullness of His time. By the Bible and the Spirit I am guarded against false or futile words.

In the third place, we need to be reminded that any doctrine, even if it pertains to the Word of God, is "unto the glory of God." When we seek to make our personal benefit the central thrust of a doctrine, we place ourselves in a position of peril at the access of the enemy. He will not miss an opportunity to deceive us and we, in turn, in our deception, will deceive others. If you have discovered a precious principle from the Bible, please know that the whole point of it is the glory of God. When you begin to prostitute it for your good, you are already in the suburbs of heresy. Keep in mind that it will indeed do you good, but its central thrust is "unto the praise of His glory."

The Bible is the Word of God and becomes His Word to me as it is received and validated by His Spirit. When His "said Word" in our ears becomes His "saying Word" in our hearts, the result will be a flow of power to affect change in us, as well as all around us. Jesus said, "If ye abide in me, and my words abide in you, ye shall ask what ye will, and it shall be done unto you" (John 15:7). When the church receives this revelation, she will, as the body of Christ, come alive in this generation and do the works of Christ.

So we have observed the multi-faceted Word of God as a *Person*; as a *dynamic* in creation and history; as a *document* for us to read, quote, and obey; and as a *living entity today* which corresponds with the first three. We will seek to keep these considerations before us in harmony as we progress along the path of power. They cannot, must not, be separated. All these considerations will become valid in your mind and mine when they are part and parcel of each other.

Then, and then alone, will we see the full meaning of the phrase, the Word of God.

I consider the fourth consideration, the present-tense Word of God with power, so important that I will elaborate on it in the coming chapter.

ॐ

The great distinctive
of the Word of God with power is its "nowness."
It is our eternal contemporary.
While there is no doubt that the written Scriptures
are the words from God to us,
neither is there doubt that, in its wider sense,
the Word of God cannot be separated
from the Person of Christ.
—JRT

Chapter 5

The Word in the Now

I cannot be saved by a book, however priceless, reliable, and accurate. Its value (the Bible) lies in its ability, through the Holy Spirit, to point me to Jesus, the Living Word. The Word of God is a document but more—it is a living, creative, redeeming, and dynamic force that is the contemporary of every generation. It is the "Word of faith" of which Paul spoke when he said, "But what saith it? The word is nigh thee, even in thy mouth, and in thy heart: that is, the word of faith, which we preach" (Rom. 10:8).

The glory of the Bible does not lie in its print or its grammar; it is in the fact that it is the God-appointed beginning place of redeeming revelation as well as the gauge by which all subsequent illumination must pass. Through its stated truths the Holy Spirit activates the power of God in salvation, healing, and deliverance.

We who live several thousand years down the line from the stated truths of the Bible can live in the power of the present tense Word of God as we receive the Word and confess in accordance with its truths. The gains will be meager from all our debates on the authenticity and infallibility of the written Word of God, unless and until we discover the power of God through His Word.

It is not the Christ of the Gospels that we now know. It is the revealed Christ. Paul said, "Henceforth know we no man after the flesh . . . we have known Christ after the flesh . . . henceforth know we him no more" (2 Cor. 5:16). The manner in which we now know Him is the same as John experienced on the Isle of Patmos. John, who once had laid his head on the bosom of Jesus, now falls at His feet as one dead (Rev. 1:17). There are not two Christs, but two levels of knowledge regarding Him. The first has to do with knowing Him as a visible, natural, and personal being. The second has to do with knowing Him in the realm of the spirit through revelation. It is not a knowledge about the historical Christ that saves us; it is a knowledge of Him as revealed to our spirits through His Spirit.

Likewise, it is not the Bible as a book which is shaking the nations. It is the truth it contains, spoken afresh by the Spirit of God. We are watching unfold before our very eyes the power of the Word of God in world politics. The God who created the world by His words and the starry hosts by the breath of His mouth is speaking still and His words are shaking the world.

The voice of God sounding His Word has power:

> The voice of the LORD is powerful;
> The voice of the LORD is majestic.
> The voice of the LORD breaks the cedars . . .
> The voice of the LORD strikes with flashes of lightning.
> The voice of the LORD twists the oaks and strips the forest bare.
> —Psalm 29:4,5,7,9, NIV

That mighty voice still sounds today with visible and dramatic res_ults. The landscape of the planet is being decisively revised and this can only be explained in terms of the power of God's Word, the same powerful force which birthed the worlds!

We must allow the Bible to move out of the realm of printed factual knowledge into the realm of empowered truth. The former without the latter will intensify pharisaical tendencies. The latter could not exist without the former. Only the Holy Spirit will be able to bring us into and keep us in balance.

The Bible, as a valid presentation of the truth about God, has, since its birth, been under vicious attack. That will likely continue. There is another attack against spiritual life which is much more subtle. It centers upon the theory that God, having spoken His mind in the Scriptures, has nothing more to say. If that is true, then it follows that He has nothing more to do. Thus the quiet (and seemingly logical) conclusion is that all we have of Him with us is the Bible. It is then left up to us to interpret what He meant in what He said as well as to seek to obey with all our human effort the divine commands. It is also logical to assume that any defense of the authenticity of the Scriptures is up to us alone. One result of this assumption is a continued "holy war" among those who interpret and teach the Scriptures.

God has spoken; that is basic. God still speaks; that is vital. To believe both jeopardizes neither. What God has said is vital toward understanding what God is now saying. What God is saying is indispensable to the understanding and exercising of what God has said. God has spoken; God still speaks. Neither claim threatens the other. They are mutually necessary, mutually dependent. Without God's spoken Word recorded we have no protection, no direction; without God's speaking Word we have no dynamic. His Spirit is His breath, His voice, His power—now among us!

He is not still and He is not silent. He is speaking, and His voice, breaking through the cacophony of our verbal attacks and counterattacks, will do more to establish the authority of the Bible than years of skillful and scholarly defense. A few days of demonstration of the power of the Word of God among us will culminate in more spiritual life than all the debates of history have produced. When that power breaks over us we will, one and all, surely be on our faces in repentance and reverence. "This is the one I esteem: he who is humble and contrite in spirit, and trembles at my word" (Isa. 66:2, NIV).

I have been greatly helped in this study by listening to respected voices of the past, especially Watchman Nee and William Law.

Watchman Nee, in his book *The Ministry of the Word*, maintains a careful balance between ultimate respect for the biblical document and the work of the Holy Spirit in revelation today. He was appar-

ently keenly aware of the tension between the two and the dangers
of falling too much to one side or the other. He says,

> As we categorically deny that beyond the sixty-six books of the
> Bible someone could write a sixty-seventh book, we equally re-
> ject the notion that men today can receive revelation not found
> in the Bible or can possess a ministry additional to what the Bi-
> ble permits.
>
> If we do not hear what God has spoken in the past, we have
> no way to obtain revelation. Revelation is born out of previous
> revelation, not isolatedly given. This is the way of revelation. It is
> not a light given in isolation, but is a light which comes from
> within the Word and increases in brightness as time goes on.
> This is God's revelation. Without past revelation God's light has
> no ground on which to operate.
>
> God's revelation today cannot be given in the same as at the
> very first. When He revealed to the first man He spoke without
> there being any previous background on man's part. In the ad-
> vanced world of today, however, he speaks only on the basis of
> what he has already said. All His subsequent revelations are de-
> rived from the first one.[13]

On the other side of the issue he says,

> The ministry of the Word requires God's interpretations of God's
> written Word. He who is familiar with the Old Testament is not
> automatically enabled to write the New Testament; neither is one
> who is well versed in the New Testament necessarily competent
> as a minister of today's Word.
>
> Upon the basis of God's recorded Word there needs to be
> God's interpretation. God must explain His Own past Word to
> His minister; otherwise there can be no ministry. Just as we must
> set aside all words that have no foundation, we cannot accept
> anything that does not come from God's interpretation. God
> alone is able to explain what He has said before. A minister of
> the Word must speak according to God's former Word and with
> the interpretation of the Holy Spirit.
>
> Though the Bible was written by human hands and spoken
> through human mouths, even so, God breathed upon it and
> made it a living book. It becomes a living Word spoken by a liv-
> ing God. This is the meaning of inspiration in the Bible. There is

a word in the Bible which is beyond Greek or Hebrew or Chaldean. To know the language is one thing, but to know God's Word is a totally opposite matter. One should never deceive himself by thinking he can be a minister of God's Word if he simply reads the Bible; it is instead how he has read it. God's Word needs to be heard before him; His voice needs to be recognized.

The Bible does furnish the background of the gospel; it is the ground of God's speaking. God has indeed spoken once in the Bible. But today He must breathe upon it and quicken it. Only through revelation will the Bible become living.

The Word in the Bible and the Bible quickened today are quite distinct. What is the Word of God? It is what God is speaking today, not just what He has once spoken. Once He spoke; and so we have the past Word of God. Now, though, we need Him to breathe anew on His former Word. God's Word is more than what He once uttered; it is in addition what He says today.[14]

I believe that Watchman Nee has sounded a desperately needed word for the body of Christ today. He further observes, "Let us note that the Bible is what God has once spoken, that which the Holy Spirit has breathed upon once before. When the word of the Bible is released, some people will meet the Word of God while others may miss it completely. Yes, men can touch the physical part of the Bible without touching its spiritual counterpart."[15]

Nee continues to articulate the delicate balance between the previous Word and the fresh Word as he declares,

Inspiration means that God once breathed upon this Book the Bible. Inspiration is the foundation of the Bible. God inspired Paul to write Romans; that is, God breathed on him that he might write the letter to the Romans.

Revelation (what I have previously referred to as illumination) means that God again breathes on His Word when I read Romans two thousand years later in order that I may know it is the Word of God. Inspiration is given only once; revelation is given repeatedly. By revelation we mean that today God again breathes on His Word, the Holy Spirit imparts light to me; the anointing of the Holy Spirit is upon this Word so that once again I see what Paul saw in his day. God does something today to make alive the inspiration of yesterday. What again is revelation? Revelation occurs when God reactivates His Word by His Spirit that it may be living and full of life as at the time when it was first written. The Bible is the Word of God; God has indeed once spoken these words. But to make it alive a person must ask God to speak afresh. When God speaks again, things will happen—God's Word, light, and life will come forth. Unless there is this speaking afresh, the Bible will remain a sealed book.[16]

Nee, as no one else I have read, holds a healthy balance between a solid, healthy respect for Scripture and an openness to the speaking voice of God today. To hold to one without the balance of the other will land us either in death or heresy. It is a matter of opinion as to which is more deadly. Both dead orthodoxy and erratic heresy are enemies of grace.

On the one hand we must vow ultimate and absolute respect for the Scriptures. On the other hand we must admit that unless God breathes afresh upon the Scripture it is a dead letter. The canon of Scripture is indeed closed, but there remains room, yea a demand, for God's continued input.

The principle of God's speaking is the same as that of the resurrection. What is resurrection? It is not giving life but is life out of death. When a child is born he is not resurrected; only when a dead man comes out of the grave is there resurrection. This is the resurrection principle, quite separate from the creation principle. The first principle is according to the principle of creation, but today's ministry of the Word is different. God's Word is already here, but God must speak again. When God again puts life into the Word so as to make it alive in man, this is resurrection. Take for instance Aaron's rod which represents resurrection. All the rods in the story were at one time living, for they were made of wood. In the story, however, life has left them, so they have become dead rods. When placed before the ark, Aaron's rod alone sprouted, blossomed, and bore fruit. This is resurrection.

God's Word stands on the ground of resurrection. It is not the cutting of another rod, but the budding of the original one. Since God's Word is one and only one, no person can preach His Word if he casts aside the Bible. It is still the same rod but resurrection life has entered it. The rod must be the same one, nonetheless life must enter into it the second time. The Word is the same, yet life passes through it again and again. Only as the Word each time receives life, light, and revelation is it living. Whoever casts aside the Bible is himself rejected by God, for he has rejected the written Word of God. All Scripture is inspired by God and must therefore be respected. Without the Bible as the foundation there can be no pure faith nor revelation of God. Yet even with the Bible, man has to seek further revelation and enlightenment from God. The principle is: one inspiration but many revelations; one word but spoken repeatedly by God; one Bible but frequent anointings of the Holy Spirit.

To be effective there must be God's further mercy and renewed speaking. As a matter of fact, unless God is willing to speak, men will never hear the Word of God. It is something beyond human ability. If the Lord is silent, the speaking of all the ministers is vain. Always remember that God's Word needs to be spoken by God. The Bible is the Word of God and it requires of Him to speak again.

The work of the minister is to allow God to speak through him. He is to serve God in this spiritual realm. Ministering the Word of God and ministering theology are separated by an unbridgeable gulf. Whether God is speaking or not marks the great divide. Some speak with their mind, others in the spirit. These belong to two separate worlds. Much preaching is done in the letter of the Word. This is not the ministry of the Word. Only at the time when we receive the same anointing as the apostles did do we have the ministry of the Word. People touch the letter God uses but not the Word of God. They touch the God-inspired Bible, but not the revelation of the Holy Spirit. The effectiveness of a minister of the Word is demonstrated by his enabling the people to hear the Word of God, not the word of the Bible alone. The current trouble lies just here: many can preach on the Bible but God does not speak. A minister of the Word must minister according to the Bible—yet he needs more; he requires the revelation of the Holy Spirit.[17]

Nee's book, *The Ministry of the Word,* has been on my shelf for years. Once I began to wrestle with the tension between the printed page and the living Word, I began to understand his approach. I believe Nee has a grasp of this truth that few have ever had.

William Law had much in common with Nee. Regarding the Word of God, Law said:

> As we must beware of neglecting the Word of God, so also we must beware of resting in the mere letter without expecting through the indwelling of the Holy Spirit a real and living experience of all that the Scripture holds out to our faith. The Bible should be reverenced as doing all that words can do to bring us to God—that is, to point the way. But the life-giving power of Christ does not reside in Greek or Hebrew syntax, but in the quickening of the Holy Spirit: for "the gospel is not in word only, but in power and in much assurance of the Holy Spirit." What folly to ascribe to the letter of Scripture that power which the words themselves most plainly tell us is solely in the quickening Spirit of God.
>
> The basic error is much encouraged by the pitiful reasoning of great Bible scholars and preachers who affirm that God no longer communicates with men except through the words of Scripture. Let us put their doctrine in the letter of the text, which will best show how true or false it is. Our Lord says, "It is expedient for you that I go away, for if I go not away, the Comforter will not come unto you." [John 16:7] That is, "it is expedient that I discontinue my teaching in audible words, that you may have the written page to look at with your eyes: for if I go away, I will send written words which shall lead you into such truth of doctrine as you could not have while they were only spoken from my mouth. These will be the heavenly Comforter abiding with you—the most supreme illumination you can receive from me." According to these teachers, the fellowship that Jesus offers is nothing so extreme as the reality of the Holy Spirit actually manifesting Christ in our spirits and His word in our lives; rather it is the wonderful, heavenly, sublime, communion between our intellects and the letter of the Scripture.[18]

We need the same powerful working of the Holy Spirit today that made the apostles living examples of all they were inspired to write. In no other way can we know the reality of Christ's redemption which the early Christians daily experienced. What fuller argument is needed for this divine inspiration as beyond the poor power of mere words than the self-evident fact that the natural man is everywhere in the church singing of his love for

Jesus and calling Him Lord with his lips, while betraying Him in the world with his life! Nor could this lukewarm apostasy masquerade under the banner of Christ, except that our worship of the letter of the gospel has denied its power. Men are more concerned about who has the right doctrinal interpretation of Scripture than they are concerned with whether or not the reality of the gospel is being demonstrated in their daily lives. And all because we assume that the Holy Spirit, having finished His inspiration of apostles and prophets for the writing of Scripture, now withholds that same necessary illumination from those who today read these holy truths. Since calling Jesus Lord must be more than mere words, what could so fully oppose the Holy Spirit as the worship of the letter of Scripture that is so prevalent among Christians today? When the empty, powerless knowledge of the letter of spiritual truth is held to be the possession of the truth itself, then darkness, delusion, and death overshadow Christendom. For gospel Christianity is in its whole nature a ministration of the Spirit; it has but one life, and that is the life of God by the divine nature brought to birth and power in the believing heart. It has but one light and that is the Lamb of God. Whatever is not of and from this life and governed by the Holy Spirit in possession of the heart, call it by any name you will, is no more a part of the gospel state nor will better influence man's final end than a similar learned knowledge of secular history.

One can be so proud of his doctrinal soundness that the Holy Spirit cannot convict him of the unsoundness of his life. The Bible teacher and religious leader who gains and holds a church position through intellectual attainments and oratorical skills can be said to differ from lesser men only as the serpent differed from other beasts of the field—in that it was more subtle.

In this fallen state of the church today, the Bible scholars are everywhere given over to the self-assuming working of their own intellectual powers. Preachers and teachers come forth to play the orator with gospel mysteries as though the Kingdom of God were a kingdom of words, and not as it is in reality the inward work of the Triune God in the soul and spirit of man. Paul said that the gospel was not in word only but in the power of the Holy Spirit. But these men profess to preach the same gospel as Paul, while denying that same power of the Holy Spirit that he knew; and the gospel in their mouths has become a play on words, so that they are always studying new ways to present them. They maintain a form of godliness while denying the power thereof. The truth has become in their hands no longer the piercing sword of the Spirit of Truth but the persuasion of cleverly fashioned phrases.

In the same way the Living Word of God has died in the hands of those who profess to be its dearest friends. The Kingdom of God has become to them and to their disciples, not a matter of practical righteousness, triumphant peace, and boundless, overflowing joy in the Holy Spirit; but that kingdom consists for them in doctrinal teachings and new-found phrases about these things.

The letter of Scripture has so long been the province of intellect and reason that the difference between the opinions about words and a living divine knowledge is all but lost in the professing church. To justify the lack within his own heart of the fire of the Holy Spirit, the well-read theologian explains that the ancient way of knowing the things of God, taught and practiced by apostles and early Christians, is not for the present age. Primitive Christians indeed needed to have the fullness of the Holy Spirit's manifestation given to every man, but this was only for a time, until the completeness of the written canon of Scripture should give scholarship sufficient words to study and teach.

Behold the folly of human reasoning! For as soon as this first power and illumination as a present work among men is denied today, then nothing is left but the fleshly work of carnal wisdom of the old man. And the church of Christ has become a kingdom of scribes and Pharisees.

All the New Testament with one voice testifies that every true Christian must be indwelt by the same Spirit as were the first Christians. And in none of the New Testament can a verse be found to show that Christ intended the gifts, working, and power of the Holy Spirit to diminish in the church. Now, as surely as Christ never told His disciples to tarry at Jerusalem until the power of education or learning should come upon them, so surely did He not refer to the completed letter of Scripture when He said, "He shall give you another Comforter, that He may abide with you forever."

The letter of Scripture can direct to the doing of what it cannot perform, and give notice of a living reality that it cannot supply. It is the coming of Christ Himself as the Fulfiller of the Law and the prophets; and of His Holy Spirit as the Fulfiller and powerful inward and outward working of Christ's gospel, that alone can give the possession and life of all that which Scriptures direct us.[19]

Without apology I have quoted extensively from the classic work of William Law, *The Power of the Spirit*. I feel compelled to quote more. But before I do, a story shared by Law himself brilliantly bears out what I am saying in this chapter. Academicus, a friend of William Law, writes of himself:

When I had taken my degrees in the university, I consulted several great divines to put me in a method of studying divinity. It would take half a day to tell you the ways which my learned friends suggested.

One told that Hebrew words are all; that when the Old Testament is read thus, it becomes an open book. He recommended to me a cart load of lexicons, critics, and commentators upon the Hebrew Bible. Another solemnly suggested that the Greek Bible is the best, that it corrects the Hebrew in many places; and he referred me to a large number of books learnedly written in defense of this suggestion.

Several friends of high repute and leadership in the church told me that church history is the main matter, that I must begin with the first fathers and follow them through every age, not forgetting to diligently study the lives of Roman emperors, as striking great light into the state of the church in their times. Then I must have recourse to all the councils held and the canons made in every age; which would enable me to see with my own eyes the great corruptions of the Council of Trent.

Another, who is not very fond of ancient matters, but wholly bent upon rational Christianity, tells me that I need go no further back than the Reformation; that Calvin and Cranmer were very great men; that Chillingworth and Locke ought always to lie upon my table; that I must get an entire set of those learned volumes written against popery in King James' reign; and also be well versed in all the discourses which Mr. Boyle's and Lady

Moyer's lectures have produced. And then, he promised, I would be a match for our greatest enemies, which he warned me are popish priests and modern theists.

My tutor is very liturgical. He desired me of all things to get all the collections that I can of the ancient liturgies, all the authors that treat such matters, who, says he, are very learned and very numerous. He has been many years making observations upon them, and is now clear as to the exact times when certain little particles got entrance into the liturgies, and others were by degrees dropped. He has a friend in search of such ancient manuscript liturgies; for by the by, said he, with great concern, "I have some suspicion that our sacrament of the Lord's Supper is essentially defective for the lack of having a little water mixed with the wine."

And another learned friend told me that the Clementine Constitution is the book of books; and that all else that lies loose and scattered in the New Testament stands there in its true order and form. And though he will not say that Dr. Clarke and Mr. Winston are right, yet it might be useful to me to read all the Arian and Socinian writers, provided I stood upon my guard and did it with caution.

The last person I consulted advised me to get all the histories of the rise and progress of heresies, and of the lives and characters of the heretics. These histories, so he said, contrast the matter, bring truth and error close in view, and I should find all that collected in a few pages which would have cost me some years to get together. He also desired me to be well versed in all the casuistical writers and chief theologians, for they debate matters to the bottom, dissect every vice and virtue, and show how near they come together without touching. And this knowledge, he said, might be very useful when I come to be a parish priest.

Following the advice of all these counselors as well as I could, I lighted my candle early in the morning and put it out late at night. I had been thus laboring for some years, till Rusticus, at my first acquaintance with him, seeing my way of life, said to me, "Had you lived about seventeen hundred years ago, you had stood just in the same place as I stand now. I cannot read, and therefore, all these hundreds of thousands of doctrine and disputing books stand not in my way; they are the same to me as if they had never been. And had you lived at the time mentioned, you had just escaped them all, as I do now, because, though you are a very good reader, there were then none of them to read. Could you therefore be content to be one of the primitive Christians who lived before these writings, and who as good disciples of Christ as any have been since, you may spare all this labor."

It is easy to me, says Academicus, to tell you how much good I received from this simple instruction of honest Rusticus. What project was it, to be grasping after the knowledge of all the opinions, doctrines, disputes, heresies, schisms, and decrees which seventeen hundred years had brought forth through all the extent of the Christian world? What project this, in order to learn the reality of the power of Christ as deliverer from the evil and earthly flesh and blood, and death and hell, and to become a preacher of a new birth and life from above? For as this is the divine work of Christ, so he only is a true and able pastor who can bear a faithful testimony to this divine work of Christ in his own soul.

How plain should it have been for me to see that all this labyrinth of learned enquiry into such a dark, thorny wilderness of notions, fact, and opinions could signify no more to me now, to my own salvation, to my interest in Christ and obtaining the Holy Spirit of God, than if I had lived before it had any beginning. But the blind appetite for learning gave me no leisure to apprehend so clear a truth.

Books of divinity, indeed, I have not done with; but will esteem none to be such but those that know to the heart the inward power and redemption of Jesus Christ, through the indwelling and working of the Holy Spirit. Nor will I seek for anything from such books, but that which I ask of God in prayer: how more to abhor and resist the evil that is in my own nature, and how better to obtain the full outworking of the divine life brought forth by a supernatural birth within me. All else besides this is waste and folly.[20]

The student preparing for ministry can learn much from Law and Academicus! Law touches a nerve with the following statement:

Without the present illumination of the Holy Spirit, the Word of God must remain a dead letter to every man, no matter how intelligent or well-educated he may be. "The things of God knoweth no man, but the Spirit of God." This is telling us in the plainest terms that it is just as essential for the Holy Spirit to reveal the truth of Scripture to the reader today as it was necessary for Him to inspire the writers thereof in their day. For without the same inspiration and power of the Holy Spirit, it is no more possible for men in any age to experience the reality that is promised in the Scripture than it would have been possible for "holy men of God" to write the Scriptures without being "moved by the Holy Ghost."

Therefore to say that because we now have all the writings of Scripture complete, we no longer need the miraculous inspiration of the Spirit among men as in former days, is a degree of blindness as great as any that can be charged upon the scribes and Pharisees. How can we possibly escape their same errors; for in denying the present inspiration of the Holy Spirit, we have made the Scripture the province of the letter-learned scribe? Throughout all Scripture nothing else is aimed at or intended for man's salvation but a new birth into the divine life; nor anything hinted at as having the last power to produce it, except the life-giving Spirit of God.[21]

I have found, in writing this volume, much comfort in the words of great men who mined these great veins of truth before most of us were born. I pray that their voices, long muted by death, will sound again with authority and instruction to a confused and hungry-hearted people in days of shaking.

Late in my research I came across the splendid writings of Eugene Peterson. In his book on the Book of Revelation he says of the Scriptures:

As God's word written (scriptura) the scriptures are a great, but mixed, blessing. They are a blessing because each new generation of Christians has access to the fact that God speaks, the manner of his speaking, the results of his speaking.

The scriptures are a mixed blessing because the moment the words are written they are in danger of losing the living resonance of the spoken word and reduced to something to be looked at, studied, interpreted, but not heard personally.

From the moment that a word is written, it is separated from the voice that spoke it and is therefore depersonalized. When a word is spoken and heard, it joins the speaker and hearer into a whole relationship; when a word is written and read, it is separated into grammatical fragments and has to be reconstituted by the imagination in order to accomplish its original work. Words, separated from the person who spoke them, can be beautiful just as seashells can be beautiful; they can be interesting just as skeletons can be interesting; they can be studied with profit just as fossils can be studied with profit. But apart from the act of listening and responding, they cannot function according to the intent of the speaker. For a language in its origin and at its best is the means by which one person draws near to another person into a participating relationship. God speaks, declaring his creation and salvation so that he might believe, that is, trustingly participate in his creation of us, his salvation of us. The intent of revelation is not to inform us about God but to involve us with God.

History is full of instances of words, after being written, which lost their voice and became nouns to be etymologized, verbs to be parsed, adjectives to be admired, adverbs to be discussed. Scripture has never been exempt from that fate. Some of Jesus' sharpest disagreements were with the scribes and Pharisees, the persons in the first century who knew the words of scripture but heard the voice of God not at all. They had an extensive and meticulous knowledge of scripture. They revered it. They memorized it. They used it to regulate every detail of life. So why did Jesus excorciate them? Because the words were studied and not heard. For them the scriptures had become a book to use, not a means by which to listen to God. They isolated the book from the divine act of speaking the covenantal commands and gospel promises. They separated the book from the human act of hearing which would become believing, following, and loving. *Printer's ink became embalming fluid.* [Emphasis mine]

The subtlest and most common attack in the satanic assault on God's ways among us is a subversion of the word. This subversion unobtrusively disengages our imagination from God's word and gets us to think of it as something wonderful in print, at the same time that it dulls any awareness that it is spoken by a living God. It has been an enormously successful strategy: millions of people use the Bible in which they so devoutly believe to condemn people whom they do not approve; millions more read the word of God daily and within ten minutes are speaking words to spouses, neighbors, children, and colleagues that are contemptuous, irritable, manipulative, and misleading. How does this happen? How is it possible for people who give so much attention to the word of God, to remain so unaffected by it? Not surely, through unbelief, but through lack of imagination: the Enemy has subverted the spoken word into an ink word. The moment that happens, the imagination atrophies and living words flatten unto book words. No matter that the words are believed to be true, they are not voiced words—Spirit-voiced and faith-heard—and so are not answered. They go through the minds of readers like water through a pipe.[22]

May we do all in our power today to escape the charge the Sadducees drew from Jesus when He said, "Ye do err, not knowing the scriptures, nor the power of God" (Matt. 22:29). Possessing both a knowledge of Scripture and the power of God is a necessity for the body of Christ today. They do not stand in opposition to each other but in wonderful complementing harmony. It is not ours to emphasize one over the other but to pursue both and allow them to join as great rivers into one mighty, rushing torrent. The world, the flesh, and the devil are ill-equipped to effectively oppose such a deluge.

In summary, the Word of God with power is all that God has said and is saying in Christ, in Scripture, and in our hearts brought into the realm of the present.

The Word of God with power is now!

As in all else,
the central issue of Mary's situation
was the Word of God,
its authenticity, reliability, and ability.
She heard it; she received it; she confessed it;
and she obeyed it.
Thus cooperating with God,
she became the human agent God used
through whom the Word became flesh
and dwelt among us.

—JRT

Chapter 6

Mary's Episode: A Model

The first chapter of Luke is the scene of two angelic visitations. The angel's name is Gabriel, apparently God's special messenger-angel. His first appearance is to Zacharias, a priest in the temple of the Lord. Zacharias' wife was Elizabeth, a direct descendant of Aaron. Both are described as "righteous before God, walking in all the commandments and ordinances of the Lord blameless" (Luke 1:6).

Zacharias: Model of the Wrong Response to the Word

We are dealing in this chapter with Mary as the model for the proper response to the Word of God. First, though, let us examine Zacharias by way of contrast. Zacharias and Elizabeth had been praying for a son during their early years together, but their prayers were now muted due to their advanced age.

One day, during his shift in the service of the temple, Zacharias was visited by Gabriel, the angel of God. The message was shocking. Zacharias and his wife would have a son; his name would be John; he would give his parents joy and gladness; many would rejoice at his birth; he would be great in the sight of the Lord, drink neither wine nor strong drink, and be filled with the Holy Spirit from birth. He would be the occasion of many turning to the Lord and would go before the Lord in the spirit and power of Elijah, turning the hearts of the fathers to their children, and the disobedient to the wisdom of the righteous. He would make ready a people prepared for the Lord (Luke 1:13-17).

Zacharias' response was humanly predictable but woefully short of the expectations of Gabriel. "How can I be sure of this? I am an old man and my wife is well along in years" (Luke 1:18, NIV). The quick reply and the ensuing actions of the angel revealed that Zacharias had not responded correctly.

> I am Gabriel. I stand in the presence of God, and I have been sent to speak to you and to tell you this good news. And now you will be silent and not able to speak until the day this happens, because you did not believe my words, which will come true at their proper time.
> —Luke 1:19-20, NIV

Zacharias finished his shift in the temple and was unable to speak as he went to his house. It wasn't long before Elizabeth was pregnant! I have read that story for all the years of my Christian life. Several things were obvious to me. Zacharias and Elizabeth had prayed for a son, but she was barren. They surely had long since given up hope and ceased their praying. Zacharias was shocked when the angel informed him that their prayers had been heard and would be answered. In fact, he expressed doubt and got himself into trouble.

When I began to study the Word of God with a view of its power, I was startled one day in the pulpit as I preached on this episode. It dawned on me why the angel struck Zacharias mute. I had assumed that this was an act of anger and judgment. Not at all! It was an act of mercy. The mouth of Zacharias would have stood in the way of God's plan. Can you imagine what he might have said when he got home that day had he been able to talk?

"Elizabeth, you won't believe what happened at church today!"

"Yeah, right, Zacharias, what happened?"

"An angel showed up and talked to me."

"Right, and what did he say?"

"You're not going to believe it!"

"Well, try me!"

"He said you and I are going to have a baby! Isn't that a hoot? I told him that it was a long shot, since I was an old man and you were well along in years. Can you imagine anything as preposterous as that?"

As the conversation went on, Zacharias would have talked himself and Elizabeth right out of the parenting business! His mouth was hushed to protect the plan of God! How often do we follow Zacharias' example and open our mouths to speak on the basis of what we feel and see? Fortunately the Bible also gives us Mary's example.

Mary: Responding in Humility and Faith

It was the sixth month of Elizabeth's pregnancy when Gabriel made his second visit, to inform Mary, living in Nazareth, that she too would get pregnant and have a baby and He would be Jesus.

> You will be with child and give birth to a son, and you are to give him the name Jesus. He will be great and will be called the Son of the Most High. The Lord God will give him the throne of his father David, and he will reign over the house of Jacob forever; his kingdom will never end.
> —Luke 1:31-33, NIV

Mary replied with a question that seems at first similar to the one asked more than six months before by Zacharias. "How will this be . . . since I am a virgin?" (Luke 1:34, NIV). Though she viewed the promise in the light of a human problem, she expressed no doubt at the angel's word. A respectful question prompted a gentle but powerful answer:

"The Holy Spirit will come upon you, and the power of the Most High will overshadow you. So the holy one to be born will be called the Son of God" (Luke 1:35, NIV).

Gabriel further informed Mary that her relative, Elizabeth, was already pregnant and six months into motherhood. He then said something that is extremely crucial to our study. Most translations have Gabriel saying in verse 37, "For with God nothing shall be impossible." While that is indeed a true statement, the real meaning of the passage is all but obscured. The literal translation from the Greek reads: "No word *(rhema)* from God is without dynamic." Converted to the positive, the statement can be read to declare: *"Every word from God has power!"*

What was Gabriel saying? "Mary, I know you have never had sexual relations with a man. I also know you have never known a baby to be conceived without a man's help. But, Mary, if you understood the nature of God's Word, you would know when God says a thing, inherent in what He says is the power to bring it to pass!"

What Gabriel said in verse 37 is the text of this whole study and is a non-negotiable, undebatable, and unimpeachable scientific fact. *The Word of God has power!*

The word used here for "word" is *rhema*, as over against *logos*, the more popular usage. Though there is no clear-cut case for the difference in these words, it is commonly believed (and I concur) that the implication is that *logos* refers to the written word while *rhema* refers to the spoken word. While the usages of these words are not uniform as to these meanings, it seems to be a safe supposition. The word *logos* is used to denote the word 165 times as over against 26 times for *rhema*. It seems significant that in the Septuagint, the Greek translation of the Old Testament, the word *logos* predominates in the historical books, while *rhema* predominates in the prophetical books as much as eight to one.

The important thing to remember is that God's Word is not without ability. The word *adunatai* means "powerless." The word is derived from *dunamis* which means "power." Power, simply defined, is the ability to affect change or produce an effect. It is the capacity to wield force.

In Jewish thought when a person spoke a word, it was perceived to be a living thing. Once out of the speaker's mouth it became distinct from that person. It had a life source of its own though still representing the person who spoke it. As a living thing that word would, of itself, accomplish precisely what was said. When God spoke, His power was in what He had to say. So it was He, Himself, coming to them. Because the Word was one with God, it was an extension of Himself. This truth is exemplified in Isaiah 55:

As the rain and snow come down from heaven, and do not return to it without watering the earth and making it bud and

flourish, so that it yields seed for the sower and bread for the eater, so is my word that goes out of my mouth: It will not return to me empty, but will accomplish what I desire and achieve the purpose for which I sent it.
—Isaiah 55:10-11, NIV

The Word of God here is perceived as a living power with the ability to accomplish and fulfill the total purpose of God.

In another place the Word is sent to heal: "He sent his word, and healed them" (Ps. 107:20).

During this study I had the opportunity to speak with an Orthodox Jewish rabbi regarding this issue of words and the Word of God. I wanted to hear it from a totally Jewish perspective. He informed me that what I heard was true and that he believed that words are the protoplasm of the universe. God made the world out of words with His spoken Word. He even said that he believed that the letters of the Hebrew alphabet have power of themselves quite apart from the meaning of the words they comprise. Since the Bible is a Jewish book, with Jewish authors, written mainly to Jewish minds, we do well to study from a Jewish mentality.

We have previously seen the power that is in the Word of God as He spoke and created the universe in its entirety. All life is derived from His Word and all life is sustained by His Word. All things in the universe, from the atom with all its minute component parts to the largest of the galaxies, were brought into being by this Word of which the angel, Gabriel, spoke. Gabriel had been there when that power that brought light and order into chaos and darkness was unleashed. All the power in the universe is derived from the Word of God.

Let us observe how Mary was an exemplary model of the proper response to the Word of God.

First, we may assume that Mary, like her relative Elizabeth, lived in a manner so as to be constantly exposed to the Scriptures. Elizabeth, with Zacharias, was godly and careful to walk in all the laws and ordinances of God. Mary lived within proximity of the speaking voice of God. She had learned to listen!

Second, Mary heard the Word of God. She heard because she was where she could listen. My friend, Clark Whitten, says, "We do not have a *hearing* problem; we have a *listening* problem. We do not have a *seeing* problem; we have a *looking* problem." If we listen, we will hear; if we look we will see. Mary both listened and heard and looked and saw. It is not enough just to hear. Though many never hear, others hear and never heed. They are "hearers only" and not doers (Jas. 1:22).

Third, Mary received the Word of God. Her immediate reply to Gabriel was, "I am the Lord's servant" (Luke 1:38, NIV). This was Mary's way of saying, "My purpose for being alive is to serve the Lord, so I make myself available to Him."

Do you think for a moment that Mary understood this sudden turn of events? We read that story with such familiarity that we miss the pathos and drama. Do you remember that Mary was planning to be married to her sweetheart, Joseph? Are you aware that sexual promiscuity was (and still should be) looked upon as a horrible sin? And out of the blue, an angel informs her that she is going to get pregnant. Well, don't you know that she thought, *What? Pregnant? Me? What will my folks think? What about Joseph? This is just great!* She might have thought it, but she never expressed it. She received the Word in gentle, quiet faith.

A word about understanding might help here. Faith does not need to understand. Faith does not figure things out. When we hear a word from God we do not need the luxury of comprehension. We would move much farther and faster if we would abandon the necessity of having to understand before we received. So often we are moved to respond, "I am going to have to think about that." May I ask a question: "What are you going to use to think about it?" Your mind? I see, and are you aware that by the time you were ten years of age you were schooled in the best of Aristotelean learning techniques and had the mind of a typical agnostic (unless you had some powerful influences from the other direction). And you want to think about it? Mary didn't have to think about it; she merely received what she heard.

Fourth, Mary confessed the Word of God that she had received. When Mary made the articulation spoken to her by Gabriel the active Word by her vocal confession, it happened! Mary was instantaneously pregnant. I understand that conception takes place when a male seed (or sperm) is received in the female egg. In this case the seed was the Word of God. Do you remember the parable of the sower, seed, and soil? Luke 8:11 begins the explanation of the parable, "The seed is the Word of God." It is more than interesting to note that the word for "seed" is the Greek word *spermos*, from which we get our word *sperm*. Its literal meaning is "issue." It is this "issue" that is at the heart of this whole emphasis. Just as the Word of God is the central issue in creation, history, and salvation, it is central in every situation we face. What God has said and what God is saying is the bottom line of every situation.

At what precise moment did Mary become pregnant? At the exact moment that she articulated her faith. "Be it unto me according to thy word" (Luke 1:38). Whatever language she spoke, by the time the final syllable was past her lips, she was pregnant! This gives us a vital clue as to how "the Word becomes flesh" in our own experience. We were saved in the same manner. The Word of God came to us; we heard, received, and confessed. The result was instantaneous salvation. We received the seed of the Word and were impregnated with divine life. This is precisely how we are to receive His Word on anything—healing, deliverance, guidance, encouragement, or provision. As we hear the Word and receive it with confession, we get pregnant by the Word of God, pregnant with whatever the Word promised.

I was recently in a conference preaching on this process by which Mary got pregnant by the Word. A young preacher excitedly approached me after the sermon saying, "Praise the Lord! I'm going back to my church and tell my folks that I got pregnant at this conference." I knew what he meant but was not at all sure that they would know what he meant. I think I suggested that a prior explanation might be helpful. But somehow I knew the Lord could take care of it. About three weeks later I received a hand-written letter from this young preacher. He said, "When I got back to my church I decided it was not best to tell them. I just thought I would wait until I started showing!" He added, "Sure enough, it wasn't long!"

And it will not be long with you either. When the Word of God is received into your heart or mine, it has power in itself to affect what it says.

Finally, Mary obeyed the Word she had heard, received, and confessed. Her faith required no confirmation, no tests, no doctor's diagnosis. She simply knew that she knew that she knew! And she started acting on it. She put her faith in shoe leather. It says of her that she arose and went to the hill country where Elizabeth lived. She expressed belief through her actions in all the angel, Gabriel, had told her. Notice that when she arrived in Elizabeth's house the babe in Elizabeth's womb leaped. Immediately Elizabeth was filled with the Spirit and began to speak under the prompting of the Spirit:

> "Blessed are you among women, and blessed is the child you will bear! But why am I so favored, that the mother of my Lord should come to me? As soon as the sound of your greeting reached my ears, the baby in my womb leaped for joy. Blessed is she who has believed that what the Lord has said to her will be accomplished!"
> —Luke 1:42-45, NIV

Elizabeth knew nothing of this in the natural. She had received the Word in her spirit and gave it expression with her voice. Immediately upon Elizabeth's response, Mary began:

> "My soul glorifies the Lord and my spirit rejoices in God my Saviour, for he has been mindful of the humble state of his servant. From now on all generations will call me blessed, for the Mighty One has done great things for me—holy is his name. His mercy extends to those who fear him, from generation to generation. He has performed mighty deeds with his arm; he has scattered those who are proud in their inmost thoughts. He has brought down rulers from their thrones but has lifted up the humble."
> —Luke 1:46-52, NIV

No sooner had Mary put feet to her faith and gone to Elizabeth's house than she received confirmation that what God had promised was hers indeed! Her rapid obedience brought rapid confirmation of the validity of the promises. She had cooperated with the Word of God, and the Word became powerful to accomplish the will of God.

But Mary's cooperation did not stop here. "She brought forth her firstborn son, . . . and laid him in a manger" (Luke 2:7). The Word had become flesh! Life around the manger became a swirl of activity. The shepherds came telling of skies punctured by angelic voices, telling of a Savior they would find wrapped in swaddling clothes and lying in a manger. They further reported that a heavenly host appeared, praising God and saying, "Glory to God in the highest, and on earth peace, good will toward men!" (v. 14).

Mary's obedience continued as she "treasured up all these things and pondered them in her heart" (Luke 2:19, NIV). The word for "things" here is *rhema* (word). She never forgot the Word of God which she heard, received, and confessed.

Again in Luke 2:51, after the frightening experience of losing the boy Jesus in the crowd, Mary "treasured all these things (*rhema*) in her heart" (NIV). She had just heard her twelve-year-old son say, "Why were you searching for me? . . . Didn't you know I had to be in my Father's house?" (Luke 2:49, NIV). Neither Joseph nor Mary understood what He was saying. For Mary the treasure of the Word from God was more than compensation for her lack of understanding.

We know little about the life of Mary after those early days in Bethlehem. We meet her a few times with supporting evidence that she never lost sight of the Word she received from God. She was present at the site of the first miracle in Cana of Galilee. It was she who initiated the process which culminated in the miracle of turning the water into wine. She informed Jesus of the problem and said to those with him, "Do whatever he tells you" (John 2:5, NIV). She knew that He who was conceived by the Word of God could speak and His Word would have power.

We may happily assume that as Mary followed the ministry of Jesus right to the cross, she never forgot the central issue of her life from that day when heaven's messenger came to her house. That central issue was the Word of God! She modeled the proper response to the Word in hearing it, receiving it, confessing it, and obeying it.

The procedure is the same today as promises become visible reality and the Word is made flesh!

ಚಿ

If the church
by her neglect of any real doctrine of the faith
thrusts that doctrine out into isolation and contempt,
thus compelling it to become the property
of some special sect,
she need not be surprised if it loses its balance.
She has deprived it of the conserving influence
that comes from contact and communion
with other and central doctrines, and so, doomed
inevitably to irregular manifestations.
If the whole body of Christians had been faithful
to such truths as that of the second coming of Christ,
for example, we probably should never have heard of
the fanaticism of adventism and perfectionism.

—A. J. Gordon

Chapter 7

Power for Physical Healing

Until now we have discussed principles, concepts, and foundations. It is time now to build a superstructure. If the issues in the previous chapters are true, so what? How shall I revise my thinking and practice? What will I do differently? How will I be perceived as I implement these truths? Will I be weird? Will my friends think I have "gone off the deep end"? Against what dangerous extremes shall I guard myself? The answers to these questions will hopefully be answered in the pages to come.

We come to physical healing, not because it is the most important issue of this study, but because it was the issue that launched me into this study. I find also that it is the one area most readily accessible for the demonstration of the principles about which we are talking. I am happily discovering in these days of ministry that if someone can experience immediate physical healing, albeit on an elementary level, faith is released to receive more. In a recent meeting a staff member in the church where I was ministering expressed some doubt as to the validity of this attention given to healing. He was still in the throes of a severe bout with flu. I suggested that we pray that he might be healed right then. We did and he was! That experience served as a foundation for hearing and as a grid for receiving the further teachings of the week.

The most important consideration as any subject is approached is, "What does God have to say about it?" Where will we seek for what is in the mind of God? If we have placed our mentalities above the revealed Word of God, the Bible, we will likely ask our rational minds to "figure it out." But if we believe that the Bible is the authoritative, infallible, and reliable Word of God, we will consult it first. We will not begin with what we think or what our particular group teaches. We will not accept the consensus of our peer group. If we go to the Bible with an existing grid, we will seek Scriptures that agree with our way of thinking. We will look for proof texts to support our particular bias. With such leaning to begin with, any system of thought can be defended and the truth about that subject will prove illusive.

We must put our minds on a lower level than that afforded in the Bible. The Bible is not subject to my mind. My mind is subject to the Bible. I am asking God what His Word is on the subject. I am not asking my mind what I think about God's position on the matter. The last several years for me have been years of spiritual stretching. In retrospect I think that it all began when I prayed a prayer something like this:

"Lord, change my mind on any and every issue on which You and I do not now see eye to eye."

I began almost immediately to discover that much of what I had held to be absolutely true was, in fact, what I had been taught by a system, by my peer group, or a pre-existing grid. I was able to back up far enough to see the larger picture.

One of the first areas where I began to change my perspective was that of physical healing. I was frankly prejudiced against any emphasis on healing. Any study I did in the Bible on the issue was to prove that it was either not appropriate for our day or was to be practiced only in the most extreme of circumstances. My reactions had been so extreme that I found some superficial comfort when one of the healers got sick!

My background dictated that divine healing be under suspicion. There were unspoken rules which dictated its exercise. We were not to pray for the sick on Sunday; that would clutter up the order of service. Wednesday evening was the time to pray for the sick, but they were never present in the service. (They were supposed to be critically ill and beyond the hope of medical science!) If they happened to be present and asked for prayer, it was best for them not to get healed on the spot. That would cause a great deal of consternation, and the whole community would be buzzing with talk of weird things going on "down there at that church"!

I am aware of the controversy that has raged over whether or not healing is in the atonement. It remains to this day a much-discussed issue. It is not my intention to deal with that here, but I will address it. My position is that *everything is in Christ and His work, my perfection included. This does not mean, however, that I am perfect or will be in this life. It means that when the processes of my salvation are complete and I am translated into His presence, I will be perfect. The guarantee of my perfection is not keeping me from seeking in every possible way to strive toward perfection by cooperating with His Spirit in me in the sanctifying process. I am not going to abandon the idea of perfection just because it will not be wholly mine until later. All is ours in Him; much of it is already ours, still more is not yet ours.*

I shall not be completely healed until I see Him and am made like Him. Until then, I live in a body which, barring my translation in the rapture, will die. Man would say I have a terminal disease, namely, aging. I am not, however, going to abandon the goal of wholeness and healing just because I am not yet physically perfect.

There is the "now" and "not yet" to what is mine because I am His. I do not know the borders of either, but I will tell you one thing: I want all that is mine for the "now," all of it! I am weary of folks relegating to the future (or, in some cases, the past) what is mine for today. I will have a perfect body in glory, but in the meantime I want as much health as a human being can have. I am willing to leave the "not yet" for later, but I want the "now," now!

Thus I want for you and me all the healing that is ours in this time frame. I am under the impression that there has been a great deal more than we have been able to believe and receive.

I am keenly aware that not all who pray for healing are healed. I do not claim to have the answers as to why that is true. My emphasis here is on a higher subject, namely, the Word of God and its power to heal. I have come to believe that it is the will of God to heal everyone until proven otherwise by revelation or death.

I realize that to many readers' ears that statement will be heard as extreme, but I challenge you to think about it. What do you do when you are ill? You desire to get well and take measures to gain that advantage. You must believe that your desire is at one with God's desire or else you would be in rebellion desiring to get well and attempting to do so. If a person has a tendency to believe that it is God's will for him or her to be ill, that person should not seek any means to get well but cooperate with God in getting as much out of the sickness as possible. While I am smiling as I write this paragraph, I am serious in calling us to consistency in this matter. If we believe that it is generally God's will for us to be well, we will want to be and try to be well. If there is doubt about this rather important issue, there will be next to none of the measure of faith required to receive healing.

Now, let us go to the Bible, our trusted source, because in it we find what God has had to say about most issues that give us problems. If He is to speak now, it will be, in all likelihood, on the basis of what He said then. We will consider together some Scriptures which mention healing and seek to hear what God says through them. We will not seek to hear what someone says that God says. We will ask Him what He says about what He has said.

Scriptures on Healing

Praise the LORD, O my soul; all my inmost being, praise his holy name. Praise the LORD, O my soul, and forget not all his benefits—who forgives all your sins and heals all your diseases.
—Psalm 103:1-3, NIV

Some became fools through their rebellious ways and suffered affliction because of their iniquities. They loathed all food and drew near the gates of death. Then they cried to the LORD in their trouble, and he saved them from their distress. He sent forth his word and healed them; and rescued them from the grave.
—Psalm 107:17-20, NIV

My son, do not forget my teaching, but keep my commands in your heart, for they will prolong your life many years and bring you prosperity. Let love and faithfulness never leave you; bind them around your neck, write them on the tablet of your heart. Then you will win favor and a good name in the sight of God and man. Trust in the LORD with all your heart and lean not on your own understanding; in all your ways acknowledge him, and he will make your paths straight. Do not be wise in your own eyes; fear the LORD and shun evil. This will bring health to your body and nourishment to your bones.
—Proverbs 3:1-8, NIV

My son, pay attention to what I say; listen closely to my words. Do not let them out of your sight, keep them within your heart; for they are life to those who find them and health to a man's whole body.
—Proverbs 4:20-22, NIV

Surely he took up our infirmities and carried our sorrows, yet we considered him stricken by God, . . . and afflicted. But he was pierced for our transgressions, he was crushed for our iniquities; the punishment that brought us peace was upon him, and by his wounds we are healed.
—Isaiah 53:4-5, NIV

The Word continues to speak of healing in the New Testament:

When he came down from the mountainside, large crowds followed him. A man with leprosy came and knelt before him and said, "Lord, if you are willing, you can make me clean." Jesus reached out his hand and touched the man. "I am willing," he said. "Be clean!" Immediately he was cured of his leprosy.
—Matthew 8:1-3, NIV

When Jesus came into Peter's house, he saw Peter's mother-in-law lying in bed with a fever. He touched her hand and the fever left her, and she got up and began to wait on him. When evening came, many who were demon-possessed were brought to him, and he drove out the spirits with a word and healed all the sick. This was to fulfill what was spoken through the prophet Isaiah: "He took up our infirmities and carried our diseases."
—Matthew 8:14-17, NIV

Then he said to the paralytic, "Get up, take your mat and go home." And the man got up and went home.
—Matthew 9:6-7, NIV

Just then a woman who had been subject to bleeding for twelve years came up behind him and touched the edge of his cloak. She said to herself, "If I only touch his cloak, I will be healed." Jesus turned and saw her. "Take heart, daughter," he said, "your faith has healed you." And the woman was healed from that moment.
—Matthew 9:20-22, NIV

He called his twelve disciples to him and gave them authority to drive out evil spirits and to heal every disease and sickness . . . "As you go, preach this message: 'The kingdom of heaven is near.' Heal the sick, raise the dead, cleanse those who have leprosy, drive out demons. Freely you have received, freely give."
—Matthew 10:1,7,8, NIV

Is any one of you sick? He should call the elders of the church to pray over him and anoint him with oil in the name of the Lord. And the prayer offered in faith will make the sick person well; the Lord will raise him up. If he has sinned, he will be forgiven. Therefore confess your sins to each other and pray for each other so that you may be healed. The prayer of a righteous man is powerful and effective.
—James 5:14-16, NIV

Dear friend, I pray that you may enjoy health and that all may go well with you, even as your soul is getting along well.
—3 John 2, NIV

This is far from an exhaustive list of Scriptures on healing. I have purposely limited them for the sake of brevity. Would you not agree that we have a Word from God on healing? Let the Scriptures speak for themselves.

Health and healing are blessings from God. Long and healthy life are often mentioned as blessings of God upon the righteous.

The Word of God is a healing agency. Jesus healed wherever He went. He gave His disciples power to heal as well as to cast out demons and raise the dead.

Early believers were encouraged to seek healing and were instructed as to the proper procedures.

Present-day Healing and the Will of God

I have always believed in healing but not much! I was culturally set against it. The Pentecostals in the church on the hill talked a lot about healing, and I thought they were weird. After all, we had doctors who could handle most sicknesses, and they could do it without being weird.

Many times I have been asked to pray for the sick and have prayed for them with varying degrees of faith. My custom was to seek the Lord as to His will concerning their healing. I still do that but with a little more confidence that generally it is His will to do so. In fact, I assume that healing is God's will unless I have the sense that I should not pray for it. No sick person should go away without being encouraged. This is what I tell them: either God wants to heal you now or later or do something better than healing you. I really believe that. God never withholds what we ask for to give us something less than we ask.

We may safely assume that God wants the best for us and that only He knows what that is. However, we are not to remain passive in the midst of discomfort, disease, and pain. We are to ask! He will either give us what we ask or something better. We must not use the "will of God" to shield us against faith. Armed with the Word of God, which is a statement of the will of God, we are to ask in faith.

At this point I believe we lose much blessing. We ask in faith and then seek the rational realm to determine if anything happened or not. The Word of God is true, we only have to confess it! Confessing the Word of God is not to deny symptoms. Faith is not denying the illness; it is the laying hold of and confessing healing.

About seventeen years ago, while writing the book *Much More,* I was having an attack of asthma. My asthma was an inherited disorder and, since it was not life-threatening, I had never prayed for healing. I happened to be writing the chapters on the much more of faith and prayer, and suddenly I got a sense that the Lord wanted to heal me. I cannot tell you how I knew; I just knew. This was long before I was as open to the healing power of the Word of God as I am now. The Lord and I had a mental conversation: (I relate it to you as best as I remember after all these years.)

"Thank You, Lord, for Your desire to heal me. I believe You can."

"That's good, and that is faith, but not the quality of faith that is going to get your healing."

"Well, Lord, I believe You will."

"I appreciate that, and that, too, is faith but not the level of faith that is going to bring healing."

"Well, Lord, what is the level of faith that will prompt You to heal me?"

"Believe that I have healed you!"

"Well, Lord, that is all fine and good, but it is obvious to both of us that I have asthma" (as I wheezed with every breath).

"Do you believe that I desire to heal you?"

"Yes, I believe."

"Do you believe that I can heal you?"

"Yes, I believe that You can."

"Do you believe that I will?"

"Yes, I believe that You will." (I was interested in "when" but did not have the time to ask.)

"I have healed you! Do you believe this?"

"I suppose I could, Lord, if I weren't wheezing with the symptoms of asthma."

"Which are you going to believe, what I have told you, or the symptoms of the disease?"

I began to see through the haze of my world view that faith was the strongest substance there was, and that when the Word of God produced faith, it was stronger than anything else.

"Lord, I am going to believe Your Word!"

"Fine, then praise Me for healing you."

I hesitated because there was no sign that my asthma was letting up, but I mustered up enough faith to start praising Him for my healing. My asthma symptoms persisted relentlessly. I continued to thank God for my healing as my faith "waxed and waned." I was still wheezing when I started to bed. My asthma symptoms, not being the serious kind, could generally be relieved immediately by a whiff from a vial of medicine that formed a spray for my throat. During my asthma season I was never out without it if I could help it. Late that night I picked up my medicine and headed toward the bed. From within I detected a thought,

> *"If you are healed, then what do you need with that medicine?"*

> "Lord, I just thought it would be a good safety measure."

> *"Leave it on the dresser,"* He seemed to say.

I went to bed wheezing as intensely as before but praising the Lord all the while for my healing. I went to sleep and a dozen times or more was awakened by shortness of breath. Every time I was awakened I praised the Lord but had a great temptation to pick up my medicine to help Him out. I awakened the next morning breathing freely, and for seventeen years I have never had asthma again!

I don't want you to receive more from that story than is there. First, I don't want you to conclude that I actually heard the voice of God audibly and carried on a conversation with Him. I am convinced that there are often thought processes in my mind that did not originate in me and are beyond me. Since my body is the temple of the Holy Spirit we may safety conclude that this "God within" has communicative capacities. Second, don't throw away your medicine, especially if the illness is something crucial such as diabetes. I received an inner Word from God because I had been dealing with the written Word. Through the latter I was able to act on faith and receive my healing.

The passage of Scripture that has meant much to me regarding prayer and the will of God is 1 John 5:14-15:

> And this is the confidence that we have in him, that, if we ask any thing according to his will, he heareth us: And if we know that he hear us, whatsoever we ask, we know that we have the petitions that we desired of him.

There are two vital keys in this passage. They are in the form of two "ifs." The first is, "*if we ask* anything according to his will," and the second is "*if we know* he hear us." You see that night I knew that my healing was His will. Don't ask me how I knew; I just knew. My opinion, after all these years, is that as I read the written Word of God He who authored it spoke to me through it, and I knew that it was what He wanted to do. But I went one step farther than I had before; I knew that he had heard. After that I was "home free"! The same Word that told me if I prayed according to His will He would hear me, told me that if I believed He had heard, I had what I asked for. Do you see that the issue was the Word of God? In my case of healing, what God had said was counted as more credible than my symptoms, and I stood on it!

This is such a vital point I want to further illustrate it. Manley Beasley used to tell about the conversion of James S. Stewart. It happened along these lines:

James Stewart was a young Scotsman who played football (the English kind) with a passion and, though not ungodly in his ways, had no place for God in his life. His mother was a devout woman of faith and prayer and petitioned God for his salvation continuously. One day she quietly came to the conviction that it was indeed God's will to save James, and she turned her petitions to praise. Then she told James, "Son, I have some very good news for you."

"What's that?" he replied.

"You are saved!"

"Now, Mother, I am not saved. I don't intend to get saved. I am going to hell and play football." (I am not sure it was in that order but that is what he is quoted as saying.)

It did not bother Mrs. Stewart at all. She had the "latest news" and she stayed with it. She went still another step beyond this and told her prayer group that James was saved. One of them slightly misunderstood and, meeting James on the street, grabbed his hand with gladness and warmly congratulated him on his salvation experience.

"I am not saved. That's my fanatic mother. I don't want anything to do with God, your prayer group, or your Bible. I am going to hell and play football."

Three weeks went by and James was none the better and apparently not any closer to salvation than he had been. Then one day out on the football field he was knocked down. By the time he hit the ground he had called out to God for salvation and was sovereignly converted in a split second! It was almost the same as the highwayman described by John Wesley who was knocked off his horse:

"Between the saddle and the ground, he mercy sought, and mercy found!"

James ran off the football field, ran home, and ran through the house to the kitchen where his mother was preparing a meal. He grabbed her in a bear hug and said, "Mother, Mother, I have been saved! I have been saved!" With usual aplomb she quietly said, "Son, this is what I've been trying to tell you for three weeks!" She had a word from God; she stood on it; and that proved to be enough!

The issue of the *will* of God is the *Word* of God. All prayer is either *toward* the will of God or, once discovered, *from* the will of God. If we listen to a person long enough or read what he or she has to say, we will know their will. The same is true with God and us.

Here, then, is the process. We read the written Word of God and hear the "saying Word of God" in our spirits. As we, like Mary, hear it, we confess it and obey it. As that occurs we are impregnated with the seed of the Word. In due time we will be "due" for the answer, perhaps immediately! The written Word is made alive by the Spirit of God in us; we speak according to that Word; and it becomes *The Word of God with power!*

Let us look back a moment at the identification of the Word of God. It is a *Person,* Jesus in our hearts. It is also a *document,* the Bible. It is a *dynamic declaration* which was so powerful that all energy, matter, and life, light, and time were created. It is alive today in God's people. Hallelujah! The Word is alive in you and me today. It is spirit and life (John 6:63)! I read what the written Word says, and I hear God speaking through it. I stand in Jesus' name to declare the Word. It has power to generate change in every circumstance.

Now, you may be surprised when the use of the enlivened Word of God on your lips is used to bring about healing! This is the same

Word that brought the whole of creation into existence and holds the planets in their places. It is a Word of power then, and when it is given expression, it has creative power today to make a person whole.

Cancer and the Word of God

I could use any disease to illustrate what I want to say here, but I have chosen the diabolic disease of cancer. Cancer killed my father and has robbed me of some of my dearest friends. Despite millions of dollars spent on research, this dread disease relentlessly treads on through our ranks at epidemic level. Hardly a week goes by without information coming to me of another friend who has been diagnosed with cancer. Though there are many types of treatments for it, there is no cure. There are many different kinds of cancer, all of which are potentially fatal. As far as medical science is concerned, cancer is never cured, it is just "in remission" when the symptoms are absent.

Some of the greatest breakthroughs in the treatment of cancer are non-medical. Laughter has proved to be a healing medicine to many cancer patients. A popular author was healed of "terminal" cancer by watching humorous videotapes and laughing. He wrote a book entitled *The Biology of Hope*. His life was lengthened by several years, and when he died it was not of cancer. His name was Norman Cousins.

In an oncology clinic in Sarasota, Florida, the treatment of cancer is aided by the use of a "mirth mobile," a cart loaded with funny videos, tricks, and other things to make people laugh. The medical world is recognizing the value of non-medical aids in the treatment of disease, especially cancer.

When my father was diagnosed as having terminal cancer, the doctor suggested that he had about ninety days to live. I did not know then what I know now. Had we known we would not have received that report as final. We would have sought a "second opinion" from God! Had God revealed that it was his time to go, I would have gladly consented. Had He revealed otherwise, I would have stubbornly sought healing for Dad.

My father died almost exactly on schedule. The fact was that Dad and we believed the doctor's report, which, in my estimation, gave that report credibility in the physical as well as the spiritual realm. I was not surprised later when I heard a cancer radiation specialist intimate his belief that more people died of diagnoses than died of diseases! I believe that my father died of a diagnosis! My sisters, who sat with him during his last days, told me that during that time he would say, "Now what day is it [referring to the time allotted by the doctor]?" His immune system had heard the message, he had agreed with it, and it had shut down!

Let me go further into this horrid disease to illustrate the potential power of the Word of God. Cancer is a general term for the abnormal growth of cells. Our bodies are a vast collection of cells, some one hundred trillion, each of them containing twenty-three pairs of chromosomes. Winding through each pair is the double spiral of the DNA molecule, the genetic blueprint for life. The DNA, an abbreviation for deoxyribonucleic acid, is the word system of instructions built within every living cell.

Every DNA is comprised of approximately 3.3 billion individual pieces, each a complimentary pair, with each pair composed of four bases. The DNA in any cell of your one hundred trillion is sufficient, if we could "read" and obey all its instructions, to reconstruct your whole body just as it is. The information stored in one cell of your body is enough to fill one thousand six hundred-page volumes. If the DNA in one of your cells were strung out in a straight line, it would stretch from the earth to the sun and back four hundred times! The DNA is the controller and transmitter of the genetic characteristics in the chromosomes we inherit from our parents and pass on to our children.

Our chromosomes contain millions of different messages that tell the body how it should grow, function, and behave. One gene tells the stomach to make gastric juices; another tells the glands to secrete the juice when food lands in the stomach. Other genes determine the color of our eyes or instruct injured tissues to repair themselves. Still others direct the female breasts to make milk after the baby is born. Most of these genes function properly and send the right messages. As the cells receive and obey their instructions, we remain in good health with everything working as it should.

There is an incredible number of opportunities for something to go wrong in this vast network of genes, cells, glands and organs, with their nerves, impulses, and instructions. Every second there are thousands of opportunities for a wrong message to be given or a right message to be refused. When something goes wrong, a quick series of emergency instructions are sent to the healing properties resident in our bodies, mainly located in the blood which is manufactured in the marrow of our bones.

Often, when something does go wrong, a mutation occurs that alters one or more genes. These altered genes, now mutations, begin to send the wrong message down the line to the cells. A rebellious cell results and begins to grow rapidly, multiplying again and again until there are enough of them to form a lump, called a malignant tumor, or cancer!

We grow from a single fertilized egg to a perfectly formed human being in nine months, and to normal size in about sixteen years. When we are injured and need rapid repair, restoration, or replacement of damaged cells, our body turns on emergency processes. The white corpuscles in the blood, the warriors against infection, are called into duty, and many new white blood cells are conscripted to aid in the work. When healing is completed, a set of genes tells the body to "switch off." The white blood cells leave active duty and join the civilian population of red cells which preside over a normal, healthy life of cleansing and renewal.

A cancer cell does not obey the rules. It is a mutation, a maverick, a mutineer. It breaks with the word system within the cells (the DNA) which makes for health and order in a normal body. It has its own agenda and is hell-bent to do its own thing. Once they begin to grow, cancer cells divide in an uncontrolled way. Sometimes bits of malignant cells fall out of the tumor and travel rapidly to other parts of the body. They take root and grow according to the immune system's ability to mount a counterattack. If the immune system is not adequate, the cancer will spread, putting roots into surrounding tissues. The spreading of the cancer is called *metastasis*. It is essentially rebellion in the cellular structure of the body.

Although it is thought of as one disease, there are more than two hundred kinds. There is no single cause for cancer—there are many, and most students of the disease are amazed that so few people get cancer. A statement in the May 1992 issue of *Life* magazine supports this:

> The percentages are with the disease. In every human being billions and billions of cells live and die according to intricate ge-

netic instructions. Given such numbers, there are bound to be mistakes, cells, for example, that fail to die on cue. In most people wayward cells are quickly killed by the body's immune system. But in some people, a cell that is supposed to die escapes and survives. Then it is only a matter of time: One cell becomes two cells, two cells become four cells, four become eight. Thirty doublings later one cell has become a billion cells, weighs a gram and occupies a cubic centimeter of space. Ten doublings later one cell has become a two-pound tumor!

There is no disease which provides a better grid for the power of the Word of God to be demonstrated than cancer. It is violent and bent on destruction. It operates independently, is totally consumed with itself, and destroys everything in the organism unless checked.

With cancer we are talking about a communication system gone awry. There is a breakdown of the information system in the otherwise healthy body. This dread disease is interrelated to the whole communicative processes of the body.

Enter the Word of God! We know that varying forms of cancer respond to varying forms of treatment. There are radiation and chemotherapy. There are new forms of treatment being researched and experimented with every year. I want to step out on a limb and say that some of the greatest breakthroughs in medical science in our generation are going to take place when we give the Word of God its proper place in the healing processes. The time will come, I believe, when medical science will recognize the effectiveness of the spiritual technician in applying the Word of God to physiological diseases. And why not? We are discovering that cancer, as well as other disorders, responds to such treatments as hope, laughter, love, and friendship. If we believe that the Word of God has power, then in the name of consistency we should give it equal time in the treatment of physical disorders.

This is the same Word that brought all creation into existence. It is the same Word that continues to hold the universe together and directs it toward the consummation of the total purpose of God. It is the same Word that is recorded within the pages of Holy Writ.

Why should we be surprised when that Word, enlivened on the pages of the Bible by the Holy Spirit, causes faith to rise in our hearts, prompting us to speak to disease and demons? And why should we be surprised when demons, death, and disease flee from before it and do its bidding? Since God is the author of the whole human system, including the DNA, are we going to have trouble believing that the Word of God should have effect on the cells of our bodies?

I have spoken in this chapter in a narrow context of physical disease and have majored on one of these, cancer. What has been said here of cancer and the Word of God may be said of any disease and the Word of God.

This has not been an exhaustive study by any means but an attempt to help you see that the Word of God is feasible and potentially powerful in treating diseases as surely as any process developed by medical science.

If you are incredulous of this information, do me a favor and try it! Since the matter of physical healing is the most readily accessible, this is a good place to begin! Whether your disease is serious or slight, ask the Lord for light and begin to apply the Scriptures on healing by speaking them to your body and into the atmosphere around you. If your principles considered in this chapter are true, they will demonstrate themselves as valid.

The same God who spoke at the beginning still lives to speak and act in the affairs of men.

Here are some thoughts to keep in mind as you consider the Word of God and your personal health:

You are a human being in whom is divine life. That life took up residence in you the moment you were saved.

That life was initiated in you by the Word of God.

For you have been born again, not of perishable seed, but of imperishable, through the living and enduring word of God. For, "All men are like grass, and all their glory is like the flowers of the field; the grass withers and the flowers fall, but the word of the Lord stands forever." And this is the word that was preached to you.
—1 Peter 1:23-25, NIV

That Word by which you were born is a living and powerful thing in you. His living Word fills your interior atmosphere!

That Word is a strengthening Word, a health-giving Word, an encouraging Word, and a faith-producing Word.

That Word, in your heart and on your lips, is capable of affecting change and generating power. Physical healing is only a meager and elementary part of that vast power.

The subject of health and the Word of God would fill another volume. But suffice to say that there are multitudes of Old Testament Scriptures relating to rules of maintenance of the human body. One of the great medical phenomena of history is played out in the children of Israel who, in the most extreme of circumstances, stayed well by keeping the rules God gave them in the area of hygiene. He had said to them, in effect, "If you will listen to Me and keep my rules I will not allow any of these diseases which have visited the Egyptians to come upon you. For I am the Lord who heals you" (Ex. 15:26). As a result of that arrangement several million people lived together in a constantly moving encampment for years, staying healthy without drugs or doctors! When they sinned against the Word of God the contract was broken.

This simply underlines the theme of this volume, that healing, as all reality, has a single issue—the Word of God! Regarding healing, I believe it to be God's will for everyone until proven otherwise by revelation or death. Upon this premise I proceed to pray for the sick.

&

To speak of physical healing
and the ability of God to perform it
without observing the same resources available for the
mind and the emotions
is to be out of balance.
A healthy body housing a sick mind or bound
emotions is not an appealing thought.
Mental and emotional healing
may be the greatest healing
available to us today.
—JRT

Chapter 8

Power for Emotional Healing

For though we walk in the flesh, we do not war after the flesh: (for the weapons of our warfare are not carnal, but mighty through God to the pulling down of strong holds;) casting down imaginations, and every high thing that exalteth itself against the knowledge of God, and bringing into captivity every thought to the obedience of Christ; and having in a readiness to revenge all disobedience, when your obedience is fulfilled.
—2 Corinthians 10:3-6

The subject of this chapter involves a pressing need in the body of Christ—the healing of damaged emotions or soul healing. We dealt with physical healing first, not because of its importance but because it was the doorway into this study for me and has served as a valuable laboratory for the demonstration of these principles. We turn to the healing of the emotions, a much discussed and much chronicled subject in the Christian world today. Hundreds of books on inner healing are being written and read. Thousands of counselors spend most of their time counseling folks who are having difficulties coping with the complex problems of a world in the shadow of the twenty-first century.

This is a chapter about freedom. In the midst of this reading you will sense that you just might be a part of the subject matter. You are right! This is a chapter about you. The Scripture at the beginning of this chapter is, in my estimation, the greatest passage in the Bible on emotional healing and freedom. I "discovered" it more than twenty-five years ago under rather unusual circumstances.

We were having a series of meetings in our church when a young man appeared urgently seeking counsel for his troubled marriage. He came to the church just before the service of the evening was to begin. I told him that I could see him after the service that night. He attended the meeting and in the service was wonderfully and powerfully converted. The atmosphere of that meeting was heavy with conviction, and many lives were transformed. In talking with this young man after the service that night, there was no doubt about his conversion. In the days to follow he grew spiritually by leaps and bounds. He was intense and dedicated. He was curious and eager to learn. He asked questions that I was not prepared to answer. He advanced ideas I had never entertained. Having him around most of the time presented a spiritual challenge to me. I am not sure but that he thought being converted meant he should report to the church office every morning when work began. He was almost that regular.

One morning he walked into my study with a confession that he was highly dissatisfied with how he was praying for the lost. As he discussed his dilemma I became dissatisfied with how I was praying (or not praying!) for the lost. I was honest with him and suggested that we pray that God would show us how to pray for the lost.

About ten days later he walked into my study again with a grin on his face and a little tract in his hand. He reminded me that we had been praying for God to teach us how to pray for the lost and proceeded to tell me the story of how he found it (holding it all the while in his hand). He had parked his car near the shopping mall the day before and was walking toward the entrance. He looked down and on the surface of the parking lot saw a shiny little piece of paper with printing on it. His story ended here and he promptly handed me the tract. I shall never forget the moment my eyes fell on it! It was printed in bright green ink on glossy paper. There was no author or publisher specified. The title of the tract was "How I Learned to Pray for the Lost"!

I assure you that my full attention was captured! I read the tract immediately in its entirety. It was the story of a group of missionaries who were discouraged over unanswered prayers and unreached people. They, like my friend and I, were seeking wisdom on how to experience a breakthrough in praying for the lost and backsliders. They discovered two passages of Scripture. One was 2 Corinthians 10:3-6 (found at the beginning of this chapter); the other was Mark 3:27: "No man can enter into a strong man's house, and spoil his goods, except he will first bind the strong man; and then he will spoil his house."

These missionaries began to pray in the spirit of warfare against the enemy in behalf of unreached tribes, as well as backslidden relatives. The results were immediate and astounding. Barriers began to come down between the missionaries and the heathen. Backslidden people for whom they had prayed began to get right with God. Revival soon broke out in that area.[23]

I was deeply impressed with the tract and the truths it conveyed. Though suspicious because it was not published in our denominational headquarters, I could not deny that it was solidly scriptural.

The next week I was in a revival meeting with Dr. Roy Fish in Fairborn, Ohio. Since this tract was on my mind and I knew him to be an open-minded man, I shared the contents of the tract with him. He was equally impressed with the information. We agreed that it was an idea worth serious investigation. The best way we knew to find out whether or not it was valid was to try it right then and there. We agreed to stay at the church each night after everyone else had gone home. We would pray for the lost until God gave us light according to these passages. Our perception was that a person who was lost was essentially a victim of Satan, a prisoner, and that our task was to set that person free through prayer to decide for the Lord. We would feature ourselves as liberators as we lifted the names of people up before the Lord, resisting the enemy in their behalf, binding him that we might be used to spoil his goods. We would pray for a person until one of us received an impression of the identity of the stronghold in which he or she was held. We would then pray against that stronghold until there was relief. I will give you three illustrations of what happened:

We prayed for one man the first night by the name of Oscar McGraw. I had never seen him, but it was obvious that he should have been the first man for whom we prayed. He was, as I was to discover later, a willing prospect for salvation. He had been prayed for during the past revivals as long as people could remember. He generally attended every meeting at least once and had never rebuffed a witness, but he could never get himself in gear to make the big step. As we prayed for him, the Lord gave us one word, procrastination. That was it!

As we prayed for Oscar, we resisted the enemy in his behalf, came against the stronghold of procrastination, and claimed his salvation. The next evening I had been preaching a few minutes when I heard a strange sound from somewhere in the congregation. It was the sort of sound you would expect to hear from someone who had been waiting a long time and was tired of the wait, a sort of whispered whistle like "wheeeeooo"! It was noticeable and somewhat disconcerting. Every few minutes or so it was repeated, and I never was able to detect just where it was originating. I think I may have shortened the sermon because of the repeated sound. Then, when the invitation was given, a man located in the general area from which the sound was coming shot out into the aisle and down to the front into the arms of the preacher. The reaction of the crowd made it clear that this was a monumental move. When the pastor presented him I knew him to be none other than Oscar McGraw! The folks were happy, but no one was happier than Oscar. When the pastor introduced him to the church, Oscar seized the opportunity to bear his first testimony as a new believer.

"I woke up this morning under conviction and thought it would never get to be evening so I could come to church to get saved. (I suppose he thought that the church was the only place he could find Jesus!) When I got here I thought the preacher would never get through so I could come down here to get Jesus."

The sound had been coming from Oscar. He was anxious to "get Jesus." The stronghold had been "pulled down" the night before while he slept, and when he awoke it was to the conviction that he indeed needed Christ immediately!

I remember another man for whom we prayed. His name and the nature of the stronghold escape me, but we prayed for him as we had prayed for Oscar. The next day we went to visit him in his home. He opened the door before we were through knocking and indicated that he had been expecting us. He was gloriously saved within a few minutes! We had done no more than pray the words of the passage in 2 Corinthians 10:3-6.

The third case was most startling. As the visiting evangelist, I was placed in the home of a lost man for the week. His name was Lonnie Fields. He was night foreman at a cement factory and was not able to attend the evening meetings. He was a good man, loved his family, had the respect of the whole community, but he was lost. Have you heard of people who were described as "seemingly better by nature than some folks were by grace"? Well, Lonnie was such a man.

The pastor and I agreed one night to pray for Lonnie Fields until we knew the stronghold that kept him from Christ. When we had prayed a while, one of us was impressed with the word morality. His good life was standing in the way of his coming to Christ. As we prayed against this stronghold of morality with its attendant self-righteousness, we came to peace.

That night I went to my place of lodging at Lonnie's house determined to witness to him. His workday ended at midnight, and his habit was to come home, eat his final meal of the day, and then retire for the night. I waited and visited with him as he ate. We talked of his father, who had been a preacher, and his own childhood. We spoke of Christ and his need of Him, but there was no urgency on my part to try to bring him to the place of decision. We bade each a good night, and I went to my room. I remember praying myself to sleep as my mind was on Lonnie and his salvation. I awakened many times during the night praying for him.

The next morning Lonnie was up with the rest of us. He announced to his wife that he intended to join us at church that day, a weekday. That morning I did not change my sermon for Lonnie, nor did I give an invitation. As we left the church that day the pastor greeted Lonnie at the door. Lonnie said, "Well, Pastor, I took care of it today."

The pastor queried, "You took care of what?"

"I got saved!" was Lonnie's reply. It had worked again.

That week had provided a laboratory in which God had demonstrated the validity of a principle of Scripture. I have never been the same since that time. The pastor, Dr. Roy Fish, was then considering the call from Southwestern Baptist Theological Seminary to teach evangelism. He accepted that call shortly thereafter and has been in that position ever since.

I came back from that meeting deeply impressed with the truths we had learned about spiritual strongholds. As I pondered this newfound truth, I began to think of believers, including myself, who were in bondage in various areas of their lives. If there were strongholds in the lives of lost people, what about strongholds in the lives of the saved? Before long I was convicted that it was through the use of strongholds that Satan and his demons did their greatest work. I began to proceed on that basis in my own life.

I began with an obvious stronghold with which I had contended as long as I could remember. I had tried everything I knew to get over it, around it or through it, but to no avail. I dealt with it as a stronghold and began to see immediate results. Other areas of my life came under scrutiny and then to eventual liberation.

Since then I have seen literally hundreds of people begin their walk toward freedom as strongholds in their lives have been identified and pulled down. Not only have I witnessed strongholds being dealt with on the spot but the Word being received at such a level as to form a grid for dealing with other strongholds in that person's life. Of course, the next step after liberation begins is the ministry of liberation in other people's lives!

Old Testament Illustrations

The history of the children of Israel from Egypt to Canaan and beyond occupies a major place in the writings of the Old Testament. After hundreds of years of captivity in Egypt, their God-appointed destiny on hold, they were led from bondage to freedom. In a couple of years, after a detour by Sinai to receive the law from God that would dictate their behavior in the new land, they came to the borders of that lovely land.

It was verdant and fruitful but occupied by giants. After an investigation by a ways-and-means committee and a ten-to-two vote against going in, the people turned back toward the wilderness. There they spent almost forty years in circuitous wandering.

After Moses died and Joshua was appointed as their leader, they entered the land of Canaan from the east across the Jordan River with the help of a divine miracle. The land was all theirs in the Lord's pleasure, but many kings and kingdoms inhabited its borders. After the victory at Jericho and the stutter-step at Ai, the children of Israel set themselves to take the land. The record reads:

> Now when all the kings west of the Jordan heard about these things—those in the hill country, in the western foothills, and along the entire coast of the Great Sea as far as Lebanon (the kings of the Hittites, Amorites, Canaanites, Perizzites, Hivites, and Jebusites)—they came together to make war against Joshua and Israel.
>
> —Joshua 9:1-2, NIV

The following chapters of Joshua record the ensuing battles fought by Joshua and his followers to take the land that was theirs by divine right. After dealing with the kings of Jerusalem, Hebron, Jarmuth, Lachish, and Eglon, and crushing their armies, General Joshua and his army began the great northern campaign. During that campaign they dealt with twenty-six other kings and kingdoms, defeating their armies, killing their kings, destroying their cities, and clearing out their strongholds.

The land was theirs when they entered, but there were strongholds with strong men in charge, blocking their progress toward appropriating what was theirs. We, like the land of Canaan, belonged to the Lord, body, soul, and spirit from the moment we were saved. But alas, much of our lives was occupied by pockets of resistance, concepts, habits, thought systems, anticipations, and the like.

Paul links us to the children of Israel in 1 Corinthians 10:6, 11: "Now these things were our examples, to the intent we should not lust after evil things, as they also lusted . . . All these things happened unto them for examples: and they are written for our admonition, upon whom the ends of the world are come."

The examples of this historical period are many and obvious. The paramount truth to remember is that growth and victory for the Israelites took place in obedience to the instructions from God. Our experience will be the same.

Preconceptions That Are Valuable

It is difficult to avoid the problem of preconceived notions. Thus it is extremely helpful to adopt correct and valid ideas at the outset. I stated at the first of this chapter that the reader might sense that he or she was the subject matter. That may be an accurate notion! I want you to listen to the following statements. I suggest that, for effect, you read them aloud:

All of God's people have strongholds. This is the leading cause of emotional disorders and is a great hindrance to balanced growth in the spiritual life.

No one of us is as free as he or she can be. We might be more free than ever before, but there is always more. The bondage may be ever so subtle, but it is there and needs to be broken.

No one of us is as free as he or she wants to be. Within all of us is that longing to be free. Something inherent in the human psyche is homesick for liberty, and the yearning will never cease until we are totally free.

None are as free as Jesus died to make them. Jesus came with the appointed ministry to "proclaim liberty to the captives, and the opening of the prison to them that are bound" (Isa. 61:1). This is our legal inheritance!

No one of us (including the author!) is as free as he or she is going to be when we get to end of this chapter. I have never had the experience of sharing these truths without coming to a new measure of freedom for myself, as well as seeing phenomenal liberty expressed among God's people.

Defining Strongholds

A stronghold is an area where darkness reigns. Darkness is an illustration of evil and the absence of truth. The devil and his demons do their best work under cover of darkness, where false concepts and deceit abide. The existence of darkness anywhere in our thinking is an invitation to the enemy to which he will readily respond. If there is the slightest area of our lives where the light of God's truth has not shone, the enemy is sure to make the most of it.

A stronghold is a thought pattern alien to the Word of God. In his splendid book, *The Three Battlegrounds*, Francis Frangiapane defines a stronghold as "a house made of thoughts."[24]

A stronghold is anything in us strong enough to keep us from becoming like Christ in a given area of life. Sometimes we find our progress in Christian growth repeatedly checked by a recurring thought process. That process keeps us from total victory and delays our growth. Our goal is Christ likeness, and anything that keeps us from it calls for attention.

The word in the Greek language for stronghold is *ochuros* and means "a hard place." It refers to a place on the battlefield that is an entrenchment or a fortress. As a verb it means to fortify or make firm. Anywhere there is a fixed set of ideas, a mind-set, or involuntary feelings, thoughts, and behavior out of accord with revealed truth, we may suspect the existence of strongholds.

A stronghold is a command post from which the enemy works in the surrounding areas. He may not have jurisdiction in other areas, but from the place where his ideas are accepted, he can exert influence over nearby areas in the human psyche.

A stronghold is a place where the enemy's thoughts seem more credible than ours or God's. Paul warns, "Neither give place to the devil" (Eph. 4:27). This warning makes it clear that the Christian can indeed admit the enemy to a place in his or her life and should be constantly on guard lest it happen.

A stronghold may be an arsenal of the enemy where his weapons are stored which he uses to torment and abuse the believer. Paul warns against the "wiles of the devil" and his "fiery darts" in Ephesians 6:11,16. The weapons (wiles) or darts may be stored in a compartment of our minds where darkness reigns for ready access to the enemy to rob us of peace and keep us bound.

A stronghold is a system of logic that is a lie used to perpetrate the purposes of the enemy in our lives. The following statement is of such importance that I want the reader to make special note of it, perhaps even memorizing it.

When we believe a lie from the enemy and receive it, whether by passive consent or by positive confession, we give him legal right to wrap that lie in a system of deceit that will make it look like the truth.

Read that statement over and be sensitive as the Holy Spirit reminds you how you might have cooperated with the enemy's plan to hold you in bondage in an area of your life.

It must be remembered that the devil is a liar by nature. "He was a murderer from the beginning, and abode not in the truth, because there is no truth in him. When he speaketh a lie, he speaketh of his own: for he is a liar, and the father of it" (John 8:44). He hates the truth about anything and hates anyone who holds to the truth. His purpose is to thwart the purposes of God in us by seducing us with lies and secluding us from truth. Lies and truth cannot live in the same life without confusion, conflict, and chaos.

A stronghold is in the spiritual life what cancer is in the human body. It is an area of rebellion within the spiritual cells where individual thought patterns have resisted the orders of the spiritual immune system. It is an area where thoughts have declared independence from the head and are heeding an agenda detrimental to the rest of the being.

Just as cancer is an incorrigible maverick and refuses to be checked, these thoughts stubbornly resist change and refuse to come under authority. Behind these thoughts are the devil and his demons, who are busy marketing them and deepening their roots in the believer's life.

Time is of the essence to both God and the devil. The longer the bondage is allowed to exist, the more complex the root system and the more rigid are the ideas that give the bondage a foundation. The longer a stronghold is allowed to remain, the greater are the number and powers of defense mechanisms which serve as sentries to guard against approaching liberators.

The nature of the work of the enemy is easily observed in the manner of his work throughout the years of human history. As cancer is to the human body and strongholds are to the believer's life, the devil has worked like a massive system of malignancy during the entirety of human history, with the exception of the brief time in unfallen Eden. Since that time he has sought by every method possible to weaken the world's resistance to him and to enthrone his godless ideas in every land and life on the planet.

Because of our ignorance of both his nature and his schemes, or because we have refused to be open to his existence and work, he has been allowed to install his regimes, extend his influence, and wreak his havoc everywhere in the world with little resistance from the body of Christ. This must stop, and it will stop when God's people face the truth and take their places of authority on the battle lines, informing the powers of darkness that, "We have had enough!"

Areas Where Strongholds Exist

Strongholds may be recognized in three particular areas.

The first is the *mind*. It is upon this area that we will concentrate our study of strongholds. The human mind is more amazing than the most complex computer. It is interrelated and intermingled with the emotions and the will and makes up the expressions of the human personality. The soul (mind, will, and emotions) was purposed to be dominated by the spirit, not by the senses and drives of the flesh. When man fell, his mind fell. Ordered to refrain from eating from the tree of knowledge and invited to eat from all the other trees, including the tree of life, he had a better idea, so he thought. But devastation resulted.

The second area where strongholds exist is the *church*. Because the church exists in an environment consistently alien to the ways and thoughts of God, it is strongly influenced by those hovering thoughts. Depending on its strength or weakness, awareness or ignorance regarding spiritual warfare and principles of victory, it will overcome these influences or succumb to them. The result of the latter will be that the church will simply become a slice out of its surrounding culture. What is true of its cultural environment will be true of it. We call this enculturation. If this is to be broken, the strongholds within the church must be confronted and demolished. Unless and until this happens, the greatest of our churches will experience only meager success at best and complete neutralization at worst.

The third area where we may observe strongholds is the regions around us, the *environment*. Every area of the earth is influenced by prevailing ideas, customs, traditions, and thought systems. By observing the population and their behavior we can rather accurately identify the strongholds in the region. Spiritual discernment will confirm what surface conditions suggest.

The church, filled with its own strongholds, is not likely to confront the strongholds in its surrounding areas. If it did it could not expect anything less than crushing defeat. Nor is it likely that the strongholds of the church are going to be confronted and conquered by people who themselves are littered with strongholds and seem incapable of mustering enough courage and equipment to demolish them.

Thus we are beginning where we should, in the individual mind. Here is where the march of victory will begin. Here is where the first trumpet will be blown to signal the turn of the battle. Liberated people will liberate churches; liberated churches will liberate cities; and one day, in the fullness of time, the kingdoms of this world will become the kingdom of our Lord and His Christ.

Where Strongholds Originate

Strongholds are derived from three sources. Dealing with the strongholds becomes easier as their sources are detected.

First, a stronghold may find root in experiences behind us. Our minds are storehouses of all past experiences as well as the thoughts and responses surrounding those experiences. What happened to us in our past is never the issue that brings bondage; it is how we relate to what has happened to us that will extend our bondage or facilitate our freedom. A wrong response and the failure to right it will mean that the experience will be shrouded in ideas which will be continuously damaging to our emotions. For this reason, in many cases, a repositioning with the past is necessary to achieve and maintain freedom.

Second, a stronghold may be rooted in the environment around us. Thoughts are not confined to one place or person. They are flying through the atmosphere like sound waves or video images. Just as a radio or television can pick up these transmissions, our minds are able to act as receiving sets for all sorts of information. Because the devil is the prince of the powers of the air, we may be rather certain that he intends and plots largely to control the atmosphere of this planet. Without the capacity to detect which thoughts are ours, which are God's, and which are the enemy's, we will be open prey for the demons.

Third, a stronghold may be derived from a system of error within us. The success of the devil is dependent on his ability to perpetuate systems of deceit. These may be planted in the mental system much like cancer cells in the genetic code of our bodies. Because we are dealing here primarily with the mind, this area is most important. Whether the stronghold comes from the past or the present environment, it depends for its sustenance on a system of error which has lent it credibility. It is crucial that these systems of error be detected and dealt with, because they serve to defend the presence of the enemy's influence within us.

Detecting Strongholds in Our Lives

If you have carefully read this far, you are likely ready to acknowledge and deal with some of the strongholds presently in your life. Let me suggest, that it is helpful to know how to detect strongholds. Many times we have accommodated a stronghold for so long that our personalities are identified with it. We are heard to say, "I just can't help it; that's just the way I am!" The fact is, we have been abnormal for so long we have concluded that abnormal is normal.

Often a stronghold is all but hidden among the characteristics of a personality. If there is any question, it is safest to assume the existence of a stronghold and go for its dissolution. At this point openness and vulnerability are of great importance. Be honest with yourself.

When I was a boy we had an epidemic of the "itch." It was a rash-like disorder on the feet and hands and other unmentionable areas. There were some terribly strong potions for the "itch," but the problem was that since it was socially stigmatic, no one would admit they had it. My dad was a philosopher of sorts loaded with "bottom-line logic." He suggested one day that it wasn't *having* the itch that was the shame; it was *keeping* it by stupidly refusing to admit that we had it, and thus not receiving treatment. This brought many "itchers" out of the closet where the disease could be treated. All it took was for someone to rise and say, "I've got the itch!"

It is not a shame for you to have a stronghold, but it will be a shame if you keep it. I am afraid that the "closet sufferers" are legion in the Christian faith. And the closet of secrecy is the stronghold that defends our strongholds, keeping us from deliverance.

Time and space do not allow me to mention all of the things that could be classified as strongholds. I will just mention some general categories and then some specific problems.

General Categories:

Fixations, Compulsions, Obsessions, Addictions, Fears, Anxieties, Delusions, Undiagnosable illnesses, Curses, Eating disorders, Sleeping disorders, Stress-related disorders, Prejudice systems...

Specific Problems:

Greed, Anger, Pride, Bitterness, Jealousy, Lust, Perversions, Bitterness, Resentment, Spite, Laziness, Negativism, Accusativeness, Pessimism, Failure, Irresponsibility, Self-consciousness, Intimation, Vengefulness, Grief, Regret, Dread, Cold love, Condemnation, Guilt, Lying, Confusion, Deviousness, Selfish ambition, Suspicion...

This list is far from exhaustive, but it should offer some direction in detecting strongholds.

Demolishing Strongholds

We are back at the Word of God with power. The whole system of physical diseases is a matter of communication among the billions of cells in the human body. Likewise, the myriad of emotional disorders is an issue of messages and concepts. It is literally a war of words. All of us are what we are because we have taken someone's word for what we believe. Our lives are compilations of messages received that have served to release us to the best of life or to limit the quality of life.

Since it is the issue of words that forms the basis of our bondage, it is not unreasonable to believe that right words may well be the ground of our freedom. The Word of God will yield those liberating words.

Let's return to the text in 2 Corinthians 10:3-6. This word reveals the will of God. In summary we are informed in this passage that:

➤ We are not to war in the flesh.
➤ The weapons of our warfare are mighty.
➤ Our weapons are empowered by God.
➤ Our weapons pull down strongholds.
➤ Our weapons cast down imaginations.
➤ Our weapons put down high things which are against God.
➤ Our weapons bring our thoughts into captivity to Christ.
➤ Our weapons are held in readiness to revenge all disobedience when our obedience is fulfilled.

The written Word of God gives us legal grounds for the fight for liberty. The Person of the Word is the One in whose name we will take our stand. The present-tense illumination of the Holy Spirit enables us to press the battle. The Word of God on our lips sets the captives free. The record of the saints is, "And they overcame him [the accuser] by the blood of the Lamb, and by the word of their testimony; and they loved not their lives unto the death" (Rev. 12:11).

When the lies with which Satan has deceived the world are exposed, his power is taken away. His cause is an empty sham.

An examination of our weaponry will reveal that the Word of God, the overall theme of this volume, is the basis of them all.

The blood of the Lamb is a weapon because it "makes a statement without saying a word." It lays bare the baseless accusations of Satan. We are informed of the manifold accomplishments of the blood through the written Word of God:

Through the blood we have redemption and forgiveness. "In whom we have redemption through his blood, the forgiveness of sins, according to the riches of his grace" (Eph. 1:7).

Through the blood we are justified. "Much more then, being now justified by his blood, we shall be saved from wrath through him" (Rom. 5:9).

Through the blood we are sanctified. "Wherefore Jesus also, that he might sanctify the people with his own blood, suffered without the gate" (Heb. 13:12).

Through the blood we are being cleansed. "But if we walk in the light, as he is in the light, we have fellowship one with another, and the blood of Jesus Christ his Son cleanseth us from all sin" (1 John 1:7).

Through the blood we are healed. "Who his own self bare our sins in his own body on the tree, that we, being dead to sins, should live unto righteousness: by whose stripes [blood] ye were healed" (1 Pet. 2:24).

Through the blood we are made temples of God. "What? Know ye not that your body is the temple of the Holy Ghost which is in you, which ye have of God, and ye are not your own? For ye are bought with a price [the blood of Jesus]: therefore glorify God in your body, and in your spirit, which are God's" (1 Cor. 6:19-20).

The written Word of God gives us the grounds of our authority in the spiritual realm. The Person of the Word, the Lord Jesus Christ, gives us power to exercise that authority.

The word of our testimony is our agreement with the written Word in the name of the Person of the Word. Standing with our feet on the written Word for authority, we exercise with our mouths the power of the Word in pulling down strongholds.

Now, let us proceed to use the Word to demolish strongholds. By this time you have surely identified one or more strongholds in your life. I am going to ask you to allow the Word to do three things in your soul in the next few minutes.

The Light That Exposes the Strongholds

It was the original Word from God that brought light into existence. "God said, 'Let there be light'; and there was light" (Gen. 1:3). The Word continues to bring light into our lives as He serves to discern "the thoughts and intents of the heart" (Heb. 4:12).

When there is a thought system in the life that is not in accord with the Word and the Spirit, it should be confronted. The primary confrontation begins with exposure. Jesus Christ, who lives in you as the living Word of God, is the light that exposes strongholds. "In him was life; and the life was the light of men" (John 1:4).

The Truth That Opposes the Strongholds

Jesus said, "Ye shall know the truth, and the truth shall make you free" (John 8:32). Through the agency of the truth the stronghold or system of error is exposed. That verse does not say that the truth will set us free; it says that knowing the truth will make us free.

Jesus prayed to the Father for us, "Sanctify them through thy truth: thy word is truth" (John 17:17).

The word not only exposes the stronghold; it also serves to oppose the stronghold.

The Power That Disposes of the Strongholds

This is where we do business with God and ourselves. This business is carried out on the grounds of and according to the Word.

In the Bible, the written Word of God, we have knowledge of the will of God. As we pray according to His will, we know He hears us. If we know that He hears us, we know that we have (present tense) what we ask of Him (1 John 5:14-15). What do you believe will happen if we pray against your stronghold? The will of God in written form, given vocal expression in prayer, becomes real. We will have what we say if we pray in faith what we hear Him say.

Our Part in the Liberation Process

We have observed His part in our liberation. Let us now observe ours:

First, we are to receive the light of the Word of God. The experience of walking into a darkened room can be fearful. The flip of a switch on the wall can reverse the fear. Receiving the Word of God as light exposes both the identity and the flimsy nature of that which has been accepted as bondage.

Second, we are to apply the truth of the Word of God. Exposure is only part of the process. We are to interpose the Word of God in opposition to the misinformation system which has held us in its grip.

Any belief system which opposes faith and causes bondage of any kind is a lie. For every lie there is a biblical truth which should provide a counterattack. To believe and declare that truth is to receive and apply the Word of God against the stronghold. Let us illustrate:

LIE
I've been rejected; therefore, I am unacceptable.

TRUTH
Jesus died for me; God has accepted me in Christ. I am acceptable!

LIE
I have failed; therefore, I am a failure.

TRUTH
Though I have failed, I have been redeemed from the curse and can do all things through Christ.

LIE
I am so weak and my enemy is so strong; I should give up.

TRUTH
When I am weak, His strength is perfected in my weakness.

LIE
Preaching seems profitless; no one is paying attention.

TRUTH
God's Word will not return void but will succeed in its purpose.

As we expose and oppose the lies with the Word of God, their credibility diminishes.

Third, we are to exert the truth of the Word of God. This is the act of enforcement in which the exchange is affected. The lie which has been exposed and opposed by the Word of God is now disposed of by the power of the Word.

Would you just make this declaration with me that voices our faith in the Word of God and thus strengthens our faith?

Father in heaven, I confess that I believe that Jesus Christ is the virgin-born Son of God; that He lived a sinless life and died on the cross to pay the penalty for my sins. I believe that He was buried in a tomb and arose three days later in victory over death, hell, and the grave. I believe that He ascended into heaven where He now and forever makes intercession for me. I believe that He sent His Spirit to earth as He said He would. I have trusted Him as my Savior and do now acknowledge Him as my Lord. By His name and through His blood I have been redeemed and delivered from the powers of darkness and admitted into His kingdom. Through His blood I have been forgiven, justified, and sanctified. Through His blood I am being cleansed. I have been purchased with the blood of Jesus and my body has become the temple of the Holy Spirit who lives in me.

I have a right to be free because, in fact, I am made free by His blood. I close every door I have ever opened to the enemy and cancel every agreement that I have ever made with him by willfulness or ignorance. The devil has no place in me and no power over me.

Now, Father, in Jesus' name and in the power of His blood, I expose the stronghold of _____ and oppose it by the word of His power. I declare that the weapons of my warfare are mighty to pull down strongholds, cast down imaginations, put down all high things, and bring all thoughts into captivity to Christ. I wield the powerful Word of God right now in pulling down the stronghold of _____ and declare it down by faith according to His Word. It is done! Where darkness has reigned in this area now light reigns. I am free. I will stay free by the power of the Word and the Spirit of God.

According to Galatians 5:1, I confess that I will stand fast in the liberty wherewith I have been set free and I will not be entangled again with the yoke of bondage.

You may need to read this statement over again slowly, giving time for each phrase to sink in. Repeat each statement aloud with determination and decisiveness.

Mary began to see the process of the Word becoming flesh when she confessed, "Be it unto me according to thy Word." May it be so with you now and forever.

You have confronted one stronghold. You may confront all strongholds on the same basis. The Word will prove to have power commensurate with your faith. As we determine to believe that the most credible source of information in the universe is none other than the Word of God, we will begin to experience the freedom that rightly belongs to the family of God.

&

All that was ever needed
for us to function in our God-ordained destiny
is available for us today.
To face the demands of Christlike living,
much more the demands of reaching out to a lost
world with integrity and relevance with only meager
human resources, is an unsettling thought
to say the least.
As tragic as failure is the fear of even trying. We are
apt to know both unless we believe in the words of
Martin Luther,
"The Spirit and the gifts are ours . . ."
—JRT

Chapter 9

Power and the Gifts of the Spirit

I could not have written this chapter five years ago. I would not have *read* this chapter five years ago. I walk in this area with some trepidation. It will not be possible to escape controversy with the following pages. I was counseled to omit this chapter. I could not do so.

Some will declare that I have gone too far; others, that I should have gone farther. My purpose is not to promote or prohibit the spiritual gifts. That would, first, dilute the purpose of this volume. It would also distract the reader from the essential issue. Finally, it would be needless because most of my readers are not going to be changed one way or another by a few pages of print on an alternate point of view. So relax; I am not out to change your mind—just to offer you some suggestions for your consideration.

I have grown up in an environment of religious culture that is highly suspicious of the gifts of the Spirit (as well as the person of the Spirit). My religious background brought me into unfortunate exposure to extremes in this area. I had a personal and fearful encounter with a Pentecostal influence when I was a boy. This formed a rather rigid grid in my mind through which I processed all information, not only on the gifts of the Spirit, but the person of the Holy Spirit Himself. This grid stood firm for the greater part of the next forty years. During that time my whole mind-set gravitated against openness to the third Person of the Trinity. I had no trouble loving God the Father or Jesus Christ, His Son. It was the Person of the Holy Spirit who gave me trouble. I was afraid of Him. I discovered that you cannot love someone of whom you are afraid. It wasn't just the gifts of the Spirit; it was the whole realm of the spirit world. I was uncomfortable with this whole area of reality and found reasons (excuses) in prevailing practices among the Pentecostals to react and increase my resistance.

I was frankly irritated with the insistence on the part of some that one or any of the gifts was the evidence of being filled with the Spirit. Such reactions greatly crippled my understanding of the manner of the workings of the Holy Spirit and of the vital experience of being filled with the Spirit. Ultimately my desperation with the ministry without any demonstration of power brought me to openness about the ministry of the Spirit. I hungrily devoured the classics on spiritual life and desired all that God had for me. It was success, not failure, that brought me to optimum openness.

Shortly after graduation from the seminary I was called to a church on the edge of a thriving metropolis. A country boy had come to town! I was twenty-four years of age. In four years I saw the church double in membership three times. My own stock was rising as I was on key denominational committees locally and statewide.

One day at the ripe old age of twenty-eight I realized that I had succeeded in every criteria by which my system had taught me to evaluate success. I was pastor of a growing, upper middle class congregation, had a wonderful family, good health, and driving ambition, but with all this I was personally empty. I had focused on the place where I would like to arrive at in life, only to discover that it wasn't what I thought it would be. Now, what had formerly been periodic depression became rather chronic depression. If this was all there was to the ministry, I was not sure that I could be happy living the remainder of my life in such conditions. The desperation deepened, and I soon felt that way about life in general. If this quality of life I was now experiencing was what Jesus had died for, it surely was not a bargain for Him or me!

My openness to the Person of the Holy Spirit increased, and ultimately, in one split second of time, I fell in love with Him just as I had been with the Father and the Son! I was no longer afraid of Him. I began to trust Him instead of suspecting that He would surely ruin my life and reputation if He ever got the upper hand.

A few months later my church experienced a dramatic move of God which resulted in spiritual revolution. Hundreds of people were saved, rapidly grew in the Lord, and began to walk in the power of God. We saw nightclub owners saved, burlesque dancers leave their profession to follow Christ, and hundreds of young people come to a radical commitment to Christ.

My first book, *The Key to Triumphant Living*, was a fruit of this era of spiritual renewal.

I have discovered that only the blessed, gentle ministry of the Holy Spirit can overcome prejudices and mind-sets. I was a typical conglomeration of rationale, excuses, fears, prejudices, and defense mechanisms. I still deal with some of those that were driven so deeply into my soul during the years of my youth.

The following is the report of the opening of an evangelical mind to the realm of the supernatural, specifically to the gifts of the Spirit.

We are going to be dealing with 1 Corinthians 12:1-11 as our basis for this study. In this passage the subject is the nine primary gifts of the Spirit. There are other lists of spiritual gifts in Romans 12 and Ephesians 4, but we will confine our discussion to the Corinthians passage.

God Does Not Want Us to Be Ignorant

"Now concerning spiritual gifts, brethren, I would not have you ignorant" (1 Cor. 12:1). God made the human mind with the capacity to think, deduce, learn, and grow. Innocent ignorance is something we all have experienced and continue to do so. An honest recognition of that state is the basis of most learning. But willful ignorance is another thing! It is the result of innocent ignorance being informed of the truth and not responding to the call for change.

This is where Bible preaching is a bit dangerous. It can be destructive to traditional ideas, or it can force us into greater rigidity within our traditional comfort zone.

The best way to respond to admitted ignorance is with deliberate exposure to credible sources of information.

Enter Word of God—The Bible

You may be thinking, "But I have read what the Bible has to say about it, and I am still confused!" Confusion occurs when two ideas of equal credibility struggle for dominance. Ultimately one or the other must yield. In this case I exhort you to yield to the Bible and the Spirit of God.

I have to confess at this point that I was in the ministry for more than forty years before I ever preached a series on the gifts of the Spirit. I knew what my peer group felt about the gifts of the Spirit, and I was more than faintly aware of what the denominational mindset was. But when my high view of Scripture forced me to yield to what God said on the subject, my long-existing prejudices melted. Before I preached on the spiritual gifts for the first time, I sought a vantage point from which to approach the task. I tried to lay down my own cultural fixations and pretend that I had just arrived on the planet and picked up a book on the subject, the Bible. I pretended that I had not read a commentary explaining why the gifts of the Spirit, one or all, were no longer available to twentieth-century believers. I pretended that I had never heard pulpit oratory for or against the gifts. I also determined to disregard the notion all must have all the gifts in manifestation all the time. I sought to begin at ground zero.

The "Spirituals"

Though the word "gifts" appears later in 1 Corinthians 12, it does not appear in verse 1 in most translations. It should be read literally, "Now concerning spiritual gifts (*pneumatikos*), brethren, I would not have you ignorant" (1 Cor. 12:1). This is of more than passing significance. The word *pneuma* is the Greek for "spirit" and is used to describe evil spirits, angel spirits, and human spirits. In the *King James Version* the Holy Spirit is often referred to as the

Holy "Ghost." In its English usage the word denotes air or wind. Pneumatics is that branch of mechanics that deals with the mechanical properties of gases. For our purpose in this usage, we will recognize it to refer to real, but unseen, spiritual influences. The evangelical mentality seems to have an inherent problem with the term "supernatural." Radical, off-the-wall visions are conjured up with its mention, so I will use other words to alternate with it for clarification.

Lordship: The Foundation

The foundation to this whole realm of "spirituals" is the lordship of Jesus Christ. Only through the Person of the Holy Spirit (*pneuma,* or real, but unseen spiritual influence) can we know and say that Jesus Christ is Lord. Please remember that at no time will we be separated from the personality of the Trinity. God does not just give gifts; He gives the Spirit who possesses the gifts and who bestows them as He chooses.

When Jesus was exalted to the right hand of the Father, the Holy Spirit formally began His earthly ministry: "Exalted to the right hand of God, he has received from the Father the promised Holy Spirit and has poured out what you now see and hear" (Acts 2:33, NIV).

It was Jesus who sent the Spirit from heaven. It is Jesus who is at this present moment interceding for us. It is Jesus who is orchestrating the whole affair from His vantage point of lordship. He is doing what He purposed to do when He said, "Upon this rock [His essential identity] I will build my church" (Matt. 16:18). All that He has done in the world since that time has been in line with that pursuit. Every part of His work is vital. It was essential during the days of His earthly ministry that He utilize all the authority, equipment, and gifts available to Him from the Father. It is just as essential that His body on earth today, the church, have access to and full use of all that God has for it.

What Are the Gifts of the Spirit?

Has it ever amazed you how much can be derived from merely examining the words in a particular reference?

These are gifts. The word for gifts is a derivative of "grace." They are gracelets. They are granted on the basis of divine favor, not spiritual performance or prominence. They are given, not earned. They are bestowed, not bought. They are conferred, not sought. It would be as inappropriate to attempt to earn them, buy them, or seek them as it is to refuse them. They are in the possession of the omniscient Spirit of God who distributes them as He wills.

The possession and use of these gifts are not to be displayed like a stripe on a soldier's sleeve or a medal on a warrior's chest. A gift is something to be accepted and put to its intended use.

These are gifts of the Spirit. They are not human gifts. They are not highly developed human abilities. They belong to that transcendent realm beyond the natural. (Shall we use the word?) They are *supernatural*. They are not weird as in eerie, odd, strange, erratic or outlandish. They are spiritual, unseen, and real.

Repeat the phrase "gifts of the Spirit" slowly about five times, savoring each word. Shove aside pre-existing notions of former exposures and visions and let the words sink in. There are available from the unseen realm, gifts which are granted to us from a person, the Holy Spirit.

There are serious social implications associated with refusing gifts offered by friends or others. Refusing gifts is not acceptable behavior unless there is a good reason. It is even more unacceptable in the spiritual realm to refuse gifts offered by the Holy Spirit.

I am always coming to that place where my strength, intelligence, and resources play out. I have no more to give, nothing else to say, no more words to pray. I know only what a human being can know. I can do only what a human being can do. I can see only what a human personality can see. My work and ministry demand far more than the best that my knowledge and ability can supply. Every day I am slammed up against the borders of my intelligence, and I have to say, "I don't know!" Just as often do I have to admit, at least inwardly, "Lord, this is beyond my ability; I just can't do it!"

When we come to the borders of our intelligence and abilities, we generally do one of two things. We either quietly settle with the best of what we know and are able to do, or we will look for something outside this world system. If it is the former, we will develop, because of demands for consistency, a practical theology which makes peace with the best of human effort. If it is the latter, we will walk into that transcendent realm of the spirit and draw from it both the know-how and the can-do needed for the situation.

How wonderful that, through God's Spirit, we can expect to know more than we can know as human beings and expect to be able to do more than we could do as human beings.

Since the gifts of the Spirit come from a realm outside this visible world, we may view them as gateways on the border between the physical (or natural) and the spiritual (or supernatural). If the gifts of the spirit, from our perspective, are gateways into the realm of the supernatural, then surely from God's point of view they are gateways into the realm of the natural. Though God is everywhere and helps in many ways, there are times when a special capacity is required. *The Living Bible* refers to the "special abilities the Holy Spirit gives." Just as God must be delighted to enter into our circumstances in special ways as situations demand, so should we look with excitement upon those times when our deficient human intelligence and abilities are presented with the power of the Holy Spirit bestowing His gracelets.

The gifts of the Spirit are avenues for the coming of the power of God into our lives. He promised us power and power inevitably has manifestations. The purpose of power is to generate change. That power is ours as we are open to the endowments of the Spirit. During the last days of His ministry Jesus said, "And, behold, I send the promise of my Father upon you: but tarry ye in the city of Jerusalem, until ye be endued with power from on high" (Luke 24:49). Then, just before He left, He promised: "But ye shall receive power, after that the Holy Ghost is come upon you" (Acts 1:8).

The works of God in power begin at the point where we cease to trust in our own abilities. Jesus lived comfortably as a natural person with supernatural capacities. He was comfortable with both worlds. The more comfortable we are with Him, the more comfortable we will be with the realm beyond the natural where miracles are expected.

These pages of perspectives and presuppositions are entirely as valuable as the actual study of the gifts themselves.

The Gifts of the Spirit: An Overview

There are nine primary gifts mentioned in our passage. They are in the order given: Word of wisdom, Word of knowledge, Working of miracles, Faith, Gifts of healings, Prophecy, Discerning of spirits, Tongues, and Interpretation of tongues.

Look again at the list. These are gifts from beyond! They are special abilities that take us beyond our knowledge and capacities. Do not make the mistake of perceiving them as elevated human abilities, though all of them have a counterpart in the natural. Heightened endowments of any one of these on the human level still fall short of the transcendent capacity of a gift of the Spirit.

These gifts are given by the Spirit, operate in faith, and are regulated by love. There are three revelation gifts:

Word of wisdom. The God-given ability to know what to do about what we know. It is related to the gift of a word of knowledge as an extension. In the natural realm many people have knowledge but not wisdom.

Word of knowledge. The God-given capacity to know what is in God's mind on a given subject.

Discerning of spirits. The God-given capacity to differentiate between the various spirits at work in the world. The adage "It takes one to know one!" takes on new meaning when we consider His Spirit in detecting the nature of spirits in this world.

These also might be referred to as the knowing gifts. Each of these gifts is involved with words or messages of communication in situations where what we know comes up short.

Though the next gifts do not necessarily call for verbal articulation, they involve power in the Spirit. There are three power gifts:

Faith. The God-given ability to believe and cooperate with the fact that God is about to act through a word or an action. This is not an ability developed by past experiences or achieved by experience. The longer one operates in this gift the more smoothly it operates, but it is not even then a human ability honed to perfection.

Miracles. The God-given ability to carry out accomplishments beyond the normal range of the natural. A miracle is an earthly event with a heavenly explanation. No human is a miracle worker. God chooses to work miracles through some human beings.

Healings. The God-given capacity to affect healing of diseases and infirmities without natural means. There is an indication that instead of being a single gift to heal, as such, it is the healing itself that is the gift.

It is difficult to distinguish clearly between all the gifts. For instance, the gift of miracles certainly includes the gift of healing. The gifts of knowledge and wisdom lie very close to each other.

The three remaining gifts are revelation gifts:

Prophecy. The God-given ability to speak forth an utterance in a known language. It is not simply preaching forth the truth. It is a word from God to man in an understood language.

Tongues. The God-given ability to speak in a language not known by the speaker. It is not a learned or acquired ability. It is not a sign or an evidence; it is a gift. It may be easily overemphasized by either being inordinately promoted or fiercely resisted. Tongues are mentioned in two lights: one, as a means of prayer; and two, as a means of communicating with others.

Interpretation of tongues. The God-given ability to interpret (not translate) a language unknown into a message that is understood.

These last two are the most abused gifts in the list. They are abused by those who say, "You must!" as well as by those who say, "You must not!" Many great Christians have lived fully, ministered powerfully, and died peacefully without speaking in tongues.

I do not believe that the absence or presence of tongues suggests anything beyond that. Many have been mistaken on either side to suppose that tongues demonstrate whether or not one has been filled with the Spirit. I have known folks who spoke in tongues who were not filled with the Spirit, and I have known folks filled with the Spirit who did not (to my knowledge) speak in tongues.

I believe that all the spiritual gifts are available to the church today. I would cringe before the ministry in which I am engaged if I had to face it with the best of my human knowledge and human intellect and no more. Because of the gifts of the Spirit I can draw on God's ability to do more.

Relating the Gifts to the Word of God with Power

It is by the written Word of God that I am informed of the existence and availability of the nine special abilities that God has given the members of the body of Christ. These capacities are exercised in the name of the Person of the Word, the Lord Jesus Christ.

As I open my mouth in agreement with the word of testimony, power is exerted to know, do, and say at such a level as to accomplish eternal business.

The gifts of the Spirit are God's arrangements whereby we, as mere, natural mortals, may pierce the dividing line between flesh and spirit, the natural and supernatural. In their exercise the world will once again witness the Word of God with power.

It is inconceivable that Jesus would tell those who would comprise the first-century church to wait until they were endued with power from on high, yet in our day command us to go out and do the best we can without the special endowments of the Holy Spirit. It is likewise inconceivable that with the coming of that power there would be no manifestations or demonstrations of power.

The issue again is that of the Word of God. If we believe what God has said is final and unchanging, then we cannot deal with the gifts of the Spirit by seeking to align (or twist!) certain Scriptures which would suggest that the gifts of the Spirit are no longer in existence. I understand the evangelical perspective on this issue, having been a part of it for more than forty years of ministry. I have come of late to recognize gladly these special abilities as a part of the heritage of the body of Christ of which I am a member.

I cannot assume that my human abilities qualify me to operate in the ministry any more than I can assume that those whom Jesus left on earth were qualified in their human strength.

The Bible records in rather certain terms that these gifts belonged to the early church. The task of world evangelization today is impossible without such help. To suppose that we can do it by our mortal strength, plans, and ingenuity is the height either of ignorance or arrogance. It is time for us who say we believe the Bible to be the inerrant Word of an unchanging God to consent to the availability of supernatural powers offered to us for the cooperative ventures of the kingdom of God.

When Jesus delivered the Word of God, it was with power. By this we do not mean that He was just persuasive in His delivery or effective in His logic, even though He surely was. What we mean is that He operated in the power of the Spirit of God.

Through the gifts of the Spirit we discover, from our perspective, the gateways to the supernatural. At the same time, from God's perspective, the gifts of the Spirit occasion His special interventions in our affairs.

These gifts are mine—these gifts are yours!

🙖

By raising the rod of God,
Moses was confessing agreement
that God was the eternal Contemporary—
the God who is!
In that act of confessing,
the power of God was released,
the "Word became flesh"; promise became reality. It
works like that yet.

—JRT

Chapter 10

Moses and the Word's Power

A story in the Old Testament provides a fitting illustration for the message of this book. It has to do with one of the high points in the dramatic saga of Moses and the children of Israel on their trek from Egyptian bondage to the land of Canaan.

Moses was born condemned to die, guilty of two infractions the state deemed worthy of death: one, that of being born a Hebrew and two, that of being a boy. It was the new Pharaoh's crude method of population control over the rapidly growing slave population. He had tried ruthless oppression and ordering the midwives to kill all the boy babies, both without success. So Pharaoh demanded that all boy babies be thrown into the Nile.

Every Sunday School child knows the rest of the story. Moses' mother, with the edict of death hanging over her newborn, put him in a basket and hid it in the reeds along the banks of the Nile River. As providence would have it, the daughter of Pharaoh was bathing in the river and found the basket with its precious cargo. She adopted the child, using Moses' own mother as his nurse maid.

Think of it! The devil had knowledge of a promised deliverer but not specific enough knowledge to be able to target one Hebrew child. Thus his plan to kill the deliverer blew up in his face. The devil's crowd wound up paying the baby-sitting bill, the diaper bill, the education bill, and everything else! When the child was weaned he was brought to the palace and grew to manhood as the grand-son of the king. Moses received palace finery, palace education, and palace position.

Forty years later, Moses was sensitive to the oppression of his kinsmen by the Egyptians. As he observed one of the Hebrews being mistreated, Moses reacted by killing the Egyptian and hiding his body. As the news of his deed spread, Moses fled for his life to the backside of the desert and became a shepherd. For forty years the man destined by heaven to lead God's people out of bondage herded sheep; conditions back in Egypt only got worse.

God set a common bush afire near Moses to get his attention. When Moses came near the bush, God spoke to him. This encounter is described in Exodus 3:1-4. The remainder of the chapter, eighteen verses, records the dialogue between Moses and God.

> *I have surely seen the affliction of my people . . . I am come down to deliver them . . . Come now . . . and I will send thee that thou mayest bring forth my people . . .*

> They shall say . . . what is his name? What shall I say?

> *I AM THAT I AM. Say I AM sent me.*

Any other questions Moses had were muffled beneath the declarations of God's determinations:

> *I will bring you up out of the affliction of Egypt . . .*
> *I will stretch out my hand, and smite Egypt with all my wonders which I will do in the midst thereof.*

The divine plan was set, but Moses uttered one other excuse as recorded in Exodus 4:1: [But Lord, these people] will not believe me, nor hearken unto my voice: for they will say, The Lord hath not appeared unto thee. *What is that in thine hand?* (v. 2, emphasis added) was God's only reply.

The Rod of Man and the Rod of God

It was obvious what Moses held in his hand: a shepherd's rod. But that rod was soon to become the dramatic symbol of the power of God's will and Word to prevail against conditions which seemed impossible. To Moses it was nothing more than a simple shepherd's staff, cut from a stern sapling from the desert shrubbery. Yet God asked:

"What is that in thine hand?"

"A rod" (v. 2).

"Cast it on the ground" (v. 3).

Moses obeyed the command, and the rod turned into a hissing, writhing serpent. Moses jumped and took off running. The voice of God overtook the fleeing Moses:

"Moses, put forth your hand, and take it by the tail." Moses, with great trepidation, gingerly picked up the serpent by the tail. It became a rod in his hand again!

The purpose of this incident? "That they may believe that the LORD God of their fathers, the God of Abraham, the God of Isaac, and the God of Jacob, hath appeared unto thee" (Ex. 4:5).

God then performed a second miracle for good measure. He commanded Moses to put his hand into his robe. When he removed it, the hand was leprous. God then ordered him to put his hand back into his robe. When he withdrew it, the hand was as pure as the other.

These two miracles would be supportive evidence of the message of God to Moses. If the first would not work, he was to try the second. If that was not heeded, he was to take water out of the river and pour it upon the land. The water would turn to blood in the act of pouring. Moses never had to use the latter miracles. The rod took center stage.

The rod of a man had become the rod of God. Previously the rod had been the rod of an ordinary man with no more ability than was in that man's hand. It might be straight, seasoned, and strong, but it was still a human tool with no power beyond the natural. Now it had become the rod of God, a vehicle of His power. It became emblematic of the power of the will and Word of God.

In Exodus 4:17 God issued this simple command, "Thou shalt take this rod in thine hand, wherewith thou shalt do signs."

The Rod and the "I AM"

All that God had said in Exodus 3 was behind the rod Moses now held in his hand. The rod had become a powerful symbol of the declared intentions of God, a symbol of the spoken Word of God. In a manner it had become to Moses what the written Scriptures are to us today. Common human effort produced the rod. Common human words, breathed on by God, have produced the Bible. Like the rod, the Bible is straight and true. Like the rod, the Bible must be possessed with the power of God, or it has the capacity to kill, much like the serpent. Paul reminds us that "the letter kills" (2 Cor. 3:6, NIV).

The rod now belonged to God. When Moses obeyed God and began to follow Him, he became God's man in a special way. The complexion of the situation had changed. Before, it was a rod held in the hand of a man. Now, the rod and the man belonged to God. Now the rod could do what the mighty hand of God could do. It was wielded by a man who was God's man. God's rod in the hand of God's man!

This is the God who said, "I AM THAT I AM"! His will and Word were now connected with that rod. The rod was to act as a catalyst bringing earth and heaven together.

God's claim was that of the only ever-existent One, the only One who could say "I AM" eternally. "I have been I AM; I AM I AM; I will ever be I AM. Because of who I AM, I have the power to say 'I WILL.' I AM WHO I AM and I need be no other; what I AM is sufficient. There will never be an occasion when I AM is not enough!"

The "I AM-ness" of God is what made the rod such a mighty tool. That same "I AM-ness" is what makes the Word of God a mighty power today.

In the upcoming episodes we are going to see how the Word of God becomes visible reality. We are going to view the procedures by which it occurs. There are several dramatic and miraculous events around which these mighty principles gather. Each event has three modes or movements. Each set of circumstances forms a wonderful illustration of the power of God's word in every situation and how that power is released.

The Rod of God and the God of the Rod

Aaron was commanded to go into the wilderness to meet his brother Moses. Moses related the words of God to Aaron as well as the signs God had commanded. Aaron, in turn, shared the word with the elders of Israel, doing signs in the presence of the people with his own rod. Somewhere in the interchange, the power that was in Moses' rod was conferred upon the rod of Aaron.

When Moses confronted Pharaoh with the Word of God, it was promptly rejected.

"Who is the LORD, that I should obey his voice to let Israel go? I know not the LORD, neither will I let Israel go" (Ex. 5:2). He then ordered the taskmasters to increase the oppression and to make the tasks of the slaves even worse. Moses and Aaron protested against this punitive action, and the struggle was on! What Pharaoh did not know was that the battle was not between him and Moses and Aaron; it was between him and God!

Aaron responded to Pharaoh's request for a miracle by throwing down his rod which would become a snake. But Pharaoh called his own magicians who threw down their own rods. The rods of Egypt's magicians became snakes also. May the best rod win! Aaron's rod immediately swallowed up their rods. Pharaoh's heart was hardened, and he still would not listen to the Word of God!

Fair warning was given:

"The LORD God of the Hebrews hath sent me unto thee, saying, Let my people go, that they may serve me in the wilderness: and, behold, hitherto thou wouldest not hear" (Ex. 7:16).

Now watch the procedure carefully, and you will behold how the Word of God reveals the will of God by the power of God.

God says, "*I AM!*" (Ex. 7:17, emphasis added). All that God is expresses itself in that statement. "I need be no other; I do what I do because I AM WHO I AM!" He is as much I AM today as He was that day. But the great question to entertain now is, "How and when does the great I AM express Himself?" We shall see!

"And the LORD spake unto Moses, Say unto Aaron, Take thy rod, and stretch out thine hand upon the waters of Egypt, . . . and Moses and Aaron did so" (Ex. 7:19, 20).

Moses and Aaron lifted their rods to smite the waters. They were, in effect, saying, "Yes, Lord, *YOU ARE!*" Their action was an expression of faith in the spoken Word of God. They were pitting the revealed Word of God against the word of Pharaoh, just as they had against his magicians. Now the world was forced to say, as it witnessed the resulting miracle, *"HE REALLY IS!"*

These three movements will take place again and again as the Word of God is wielded in the hands of the men of God:

"I AM!"

"YOU ARE!"

"HE IS!"

Ten catastrophic plagues broke over Egypt, each one cutting a swath through the social, religious, and political structure of the nation. A study of the mythology that controlled the culture and religion of Egypt will give a hint of the character of the plagues. It was as if God deliberately designed them to discredit the gods of Egypt one by one.

One of the leading deities of Egypt had a wife with the body of a frog. When the frogs came out of the bloody waters they filled the houses of Egypt. Here a frog, there a frog, everywhere a frog! Into Pharaoh's bedchamber, in the ovens, in the kneading troughs came the frogs. No Egyptian would dare kill a frog: it might be his god's wife!

The blood and frogs were followed by the lice and the flies. Then the livestock were smitten, and every last horse, donkey, camel, cow, sheep, and goat belonging to the Egyptians died. These plagues were followed by boils on man and beast. The magicians could do nothing; the boils had broken out on them as well! Then came the hail mingled with fire, followed by the hordes of locusts.

Then came three days of darkness in which no one could see another, and no one could go out of his house. Then came the ultimate plague, the death of the firstborn son in every Egyptian family.

The children of Israel were told how to prepare for the coming of the tenth plague. They were instructed to kill a lamb, eat it along with bitter herbs, and take some of the blood and sprinkle it on the tops and sides of the doors of every Israelite house. This was the Lord's Passover. That night the Lord struck down every firstborn in Egypt but passed over every Israelite household.

The Rod of God and the Sea

Pharaoh finally relented and allowed the Hebrews to leave, but the story was not over yet. The path God chose for His people was toward the Red Sea, not on the road through Philistine country. The cloud of God's presence by day and the pillar of fire of His presence at night led them to the shores of the sea. While they paused there, Pharaoh's heart was hardened once more and he sent his chariots, horses, and troops to overtake the helpless people.

God's response was much the same as before. "The Egyptians shall know that I AM the LORD" (Ex. 14:18, emphasis added). There it is again, "I AM!"

Moses then stretched his hand over the Red Sea as if to say, "Yes, Lord, You are!" And God again responded to the exalted Word. The sea that had been created by the Word responded to the wind, itself a result of God's spoken Word.

The children of Israel marched across on dry land while the waters of the sea were held back like mighty walls on the right and left. When the Egyptian charioteers came down the path between the walls of water, the Lord told Moses to stretch his hand over the waters. At this the entire Egyptian army was swallowed by the waters with no survivors.

The watching world, then and now, was forced to say, "HE IS!"

"I AM!"

"YOU ARE!"

"HE IS!"

When the rod symbolizing the Word of God was exalted, God responded in power, and the slaves walked out of the land of bondage to freedom.

Think for a moment about the magnitude of the corporate miracle worked by the Word of God through the obedience of Moses and Aaron. A great and powerful nation was all but destroyed. Its religion was totally discredited. Its army was devastated. Its economy lay in shambles. Its labor force was gone. The Word of God had accomplished this.

But, alas, the story does not end here. No sooner had the song of deliverance died out on their lips than the Israelites begin to grumble. Their first huge obstacle was too much water; now, they were out of water.

"Why did you bring us out of Egypt to make us and our children and livestock die of thirst?" (Ex. 17:3, paraphrase).

"Lord, what am I to do with this people? They are almost ready to stone me," Moses pined (Ex. 17:4, paraphrase).

Surely God reminded Moses, "I AM! And because I AM, I CAN, AND I WILL!"

Then Moses struck the rock in obedience to the directive of the Lord. His obedience was his confession, "YES, LORD, YOU ARE!" Out of the rock gushed a flow of water sufficient to the needs of all the people and their animals.

The Word that had delivered them from centuries of bondage had now opened a fountain of provision in a hostile land. Again the rod had served as a catalyst to bring the power of God into action at the point of human needs.

Then Came Amalek

Sooner or later the sons of the flesh will always arise to contest the progress of the people of God. The first to challenge Israel were the Amalekites. Moses had become accustomed to the ways of God. He confidently delegated to Joshua the task of facing Amalek in the valley. Moses stood upon the hill with the rod of God in his hand! The battle began and as long as the rod was held high, Joshua prevailed. When the rod was lowered as Moses' arm tired, the Amalekites won. When Aaron and Hur saw the problem, they propped Moses and the rod up with a rock and stood one on each side until the battle was won! The lesson is so obvious it is almost needless to mention. The battle was won by the Word of God. Moses' response to God's Word occasioned the release of God's power. Amalek was defeated!

"I AM!"

"YES, YOU ARE!"

And the multitudes witness, "HE IS! HE REALLY IS!" The Word that had demolished the nation of Egypt, released the judgment of God upon it, opened the way of deliverance for the slaves, and produced water in the desert had conquered the foe which blocked the way to victory.

And so it ever is when the Word of God is wielded against the enemy.

What Is That in Thine Hand?

A rod? A human tool? The Scripture? Words recorded on pages of paper? A book written by men but given from God. In it God is still speaking to us. Its written words become the speaking words in our mouths, and it is the Word of God with power.

It has the power to generate change in any culture, just as it did in the ancient land of Egypt. A powerful nation was brought to its knees by the very Word of God that we hold in our hands and which lives in our hearts.

When Moses, with God's people,
From Egypt's land did flee,
Behind them was the enemy;
Before them was the sea.
The waters rolled up like a scroll,
God opened up the way . . .
AND THE GOD WHO LIVED IN MOSES' TIME,
IS JUST THE SAME TODAY.

And God awaits a people, approaching the borders of the twenty-first century, who will stand with the written Word in their hands and the living Word in their hearts and on their lips, and take the day! The issue is not the accuracy of His Word (though it is accurate) but the power of His Word. Its greatest proof lies in its power.

What is that in your hand? A Book? Your scholastic attainments, an exalted position, or a treasured relationship? Throw it down. This will be your way of saying, "Yes, Lord, You are who You are!" That confession in agreement with His Word is translated into power. Then, when the world sees the result of our cooperation with God, it will surely say, "He is!"

ॐ

*A*gain we are forcefully reminded
that in Ezekiel's case,
the issue was the Word of God—
what God has said, is saying, and will say.
Upon this and this alone
rests the outcome of any situation.

—JRT

Chapter 11

Power in Action

All of us continuously face situations which are bothersome as well as baffling. Though we are encouraged to seek safety in many counselors, there are times when even this seems to complicate the situation and intensify our anxiety. If we could only identify the central issue of our dilemma, we would have at least a solid place to begin. I am discovering that in all crises thus far in this consideration I am safe to make this conclusion: the issue of this situation is the Word of God—what God has said in the Bible, what God is saying to me through the Bible, and what He is saying to me in the midst of this situation.

I am not suggesting here that we have three separate sources of information. We have but one—the Word of God. But He chooses to convey what we need to hear at these levels. What He has said in the Scriptures is immutable (unchangeable), correct, and complete, but He is still talking about what He once said that has been written down to become our Bible. Hearing the inner voice of God in our study of the Bible is vital to genuine Christianity. The Pharisees sought to build a faith on written law alone and failed to recognize the One it was all about when He came. He reminded them that they did not have the Word of God abiding in them, though they studied the Scriptures constantly. They had stopped short of the purpose of the Scriptures, which is to reveal the Person of the Word, the Lord Jesus Christ.

We must steadfastly resist the pharisaical tendency to enthrone a written document above the living Christ, as well as the tendency to enthrone our own abilities to receive light apart from the Scripture. John Wesley's warning should be sounded to all today:

> Do not ascribe to God what is not of God. Do not readily suppose dreams, voices, impressions, visions and revelations to be of God without sufficient evidence. They may be purely natural or they may be diabolical. Try all things by the written Word and let all bow down before it.

Whatever the situations you and I are facing, we may safely assume that the significant issue is the Word of God, our receiving it and obeying it. Until this happens we lack the basic foundation for the solutions of our problems. If we do not get God's perspective and hear God's voice in the situation, we will very likely complicate it by focusing on the needs and entertaining multiple fears.

We are going to deal in this chapter with two clear examples of the power of the Word of God in action, one from the Old Testament and one from the New Testament.

Can These Bones Live?

These were the darkest days in Judah's history. For seventy years the people of God would be in Babylonian captivity. The glory of God had departed. The spiritual destiny of the nation was obscured.

Ezekiel, God's prophet during this time, had a most difficult assignment. He was to assess the situation, showing the causes of their plight, the nature of the judgment of God, and the possibilities of hope.

Again and again Ezekiel declared, "The word of the Lord came unto me saying . . ." More than once Ezekiel broke down and wept over the hopelessness of the whole situation. In chapter 37 there is a climactic confrontation. The fact that it was a vision being reported does not conceal the power of the truth in the figures involved.

A Vision of Dry Bone Valley

The landscape was covered with bones. Ezekiel asked no questions. By now he surely understood. The national situation was humanly hopeless—as hopeless as this valley of bones. A graveyard always speaks of purposes terminated, dreams unrealized, sudden tragedy having ambushed unwary souls.

Ezekiel found himself in a valley with acres and acres of dry bones. It might have been the scene of an ancient battle fought and consummated in such a manner that neither side had time to bury its dead. Ezekiel was led around in the valley to get a clear picture of the scene. His report was, "And, behold, there were very many [dry bones] in the open valley; and, lo, they were very dry" (Ezek. 37:2). I have a feeling that God gave His prophet time to get a solid impression of the nature of the surroundings.

God then broke the silence with an astounding question. "Can these bones live?" What would you have said? The answer to that question is probably the same as you are saying now about the problems you are facing. We often are apt to answer on the basis of our opinion or of the experiences of the past.

In Ezekiel's case, before the negative words escaped his lips, better judgment suddenly seized him and he said, "O Lord God, you know!" His wrong assessment might have meant the end of the conversation. What God intended to do involved Ezekiel. Had he voiced his hopelessness on the basis of his perspective, he would likely have disqualified himself from being a part of the solution. His answer, instead, opened the way for God's further speaking.

Ezekiel was commanded to preach to the bones and was told specifically what to say to them. I can imagine what might have passed through the prophet's mind during those moments.

"But Lord, they can't hear; they're dead. They can't respond, they can't move, they can't obey!" But the Word of God was to be spoken in the midst of a hopeless situation. The man of God was not told to speak about the bones but was ordered to speak to the bones. It seems easier to speak our words about the situation to man or God than to speak God's Word to the situation. He was not assigned the task of surveying the cemetery but of sounding the Word of God to the occupants.

God's will and God's Word are related much as fact and declaration are related. God's will is God's desire, His pleasure, His plan. His Word is His desire, His pleasure, and His plan put into sound. When God gives us the right to speak His Word and will, something happens. We have no right to speak otherwise.

God commanded Ezekiel to preach to the bones and told him precisely what to say:

> O ye dry bones, hear the word of the LORD. Thus saith the Lord GOD unto these bones; Behold I will cause breath to enter into you; and ye shall live: and I will lay sinews upon you, and will bring up flesh upon you, and cover you with skin, and put breath in you, and ye shall live; and ye shall know that I am the LORD.
>
> —Ezekiel 37:4-6

God's will, heretofore known only to God, was now made known to a man through God's Word. That will, revealed through His Word, was deemed more credible by Ezekiel than any apparent and prevailing conditions. Herein lies the key to the manifestations of the power of the Word of God.

What we previously observed in the story of Mary and her response to the words of Gabriel is true here also. She heard it; she received it; she confessed it; and she obeyed it. Ezekiel heard the word from God: "Again he said unto me . . ." He received, confessed, and obeyed: "So I prophesied as I was commanded . . ." In so doing he validated what God had said and the power of God came upon the Word of God through the instrumentality of the man of God. The result was the will of God was done!

If we could know what happens when we willingly take God at His word and recognize it to be both the diagnosis and the cure to the situation, we would have the key to every issue.

Let us observe the continuing process. No sooner had the words of God been sounded than dramatic events began to occur. "There was a noise, and behold a shaking, and the bones came together, bone to his bone. And when I beheld, lo, the sinews and the flesh came upon them, and the skin covered them above: but there was no breath in them" (Ezek. 37:7-8). Had God forgotten something? Was the restoration to be only partial? God was not through.

Ezekiel had been ordered previously to preach to the bones. He was then ordered to preach to the wind and again was told precisely what to say:

"Thus saith the Lord GOD; 'Come from the four winds, O breath, and breathe upon these slain, that they may live.'"

Again the prophet did as he was told and ordered the winds to give breath to the dead bodies and "they lived, and stood up upon their feet, an exceeding great army" (Ezek. 37:10).

Then God gave to His prophet the application of these events:

These bones are the whole house of Israel: behold, they say, Our bones are dried, and our hope is lost: we are cut off . . . Therefore prophesy and say unto them, Thus saith the Lord GOD; Behold, O my people, I will open your graves, and cause you to come up out of your graves, and bring you into the land of Israel. And ye shall know that I am the LORD, when I have opened your graves . . . And shall put my spirit in you, and ye shall live, and I shall place you in your own land: then shall ye know that I the LORD have spoken it, and performed it, saith the LORD.
—Ezekiel 37:11-14

The issue of this dramatic story is the Word of God. In the process of God's speaking, man's hearing, man's receiving, and man's obedience, the power of God was revealed and the will of God was done.

We must never underestimate either the accuracy or the potential of the Word of God as we hear it. Having no confidence in the flesh must never be mistaken for being apologetic about the power of His Word on our lips. In speaking God's Word after Him we walk into a transcendent realm of awesome power where His Word is supreme.

You may be facing a situation as desperate as Ezekiel's Dry Bone Valley. The prospects may seem dim and the prognosis discouraging. You may have no reason on the human side to believe that it will ever be any different. But remember that the issue is never in the visible prospects or human prognoses; it is in the Word of the living God. You owe yourself and God this priority—to hear the voice of God and act accordingly. That voice was the means by which the world began, the power which holds it together, and the guarantee that it will come to its God-appointed destiny.

The Word That Felled a Tree

From the beginning of His ministry Jesus exercised the power of God through words. He consistently modeled faith in what God said; counting God's Word was more credible than what was obvious. In Mark 11 He does more than exemplify the process of the power of the Word of God; He delegates the privilege of speaking the Word to His disciples.

Jesus, with His disciples, was coming from Bethany to Jerusalem where He would cleanse the temple. On the way He saw a fig tree with leaves, and sought for a wayside snack. Finding no fruit, He spoke less than a dozen words to consign the tree to its destiny of death. "No man eat fruit of thee hereafter for ever" (Mark 11:14). Later as they passed the same way going out of the city, Peter noticed the fig tree and said, "Master, behold the fig tree which thou cursed is withered away" (v. 21). Mark commented in verse 20 that the fig tree was dried up from the roots. The words of Jesus had terminated the life of the tree!

Jesus seized this opportunity to teach His disciples a vital truth. The *King James Version* indicates that He said, "Have faith in God" (v. 22). A literal rendering of the Greek reads, "Have the faith of God." While the first translation points to a necessary exercise, it falls short of the potential of the literal rendering. Jesus was saying they were to have the God-kind of faith or faith like God's. Does God have faith? If so, what kind of faith does He have? In what does He place His faith? The answer is, "Yes, God has faith; it is an unshakable faith in His own immutable will and Word." He exercised that faith when He created the universe by means of His Word. He has been working in a similar manner ever since.

Jesus here indicated that it was the manner in which the disciples were to operate. Read carefully His words:

> For verily I say unto you, That whosoever shall say unto this mountain, Be thou removed, and be thou cast into the sea; and shall not doubt in his heart, but shall believe that those things which he saith shall come to pass; he shall have whatsoever he saith.
>
> —Mark 11:23

Believers have been discussing that narrative ever since it happened. Some have sought to revise it to mean something less than it really means, while others have found in it a license to go around saying anything that a whim arouses with the hope that it will happen. A few have examined it and allowed it to say what it means. Nowhere is the example and teaching of how the Word of God operates any clearer than in this passage.

The action of Jesus, as mysterious as it is, can only be understood as a platform for the teaching of a vital principle. He practiced the God-kind of faith mentioned by the psalmist: "For he spake, and it was done . . ." (Ps. 33:9). Jesus spoke according to the will of God and power was released that terminated the life system of the true. The words of Jesus had power to generate change!

The crucial issue of the passage in Mark as it relates to the disciples is found in the words, "For verily I say unto you . . ." (v. 23). We are to speak according to His speaking. We cannot expect other words to be the occasion of the release of the power of God. But when He says something to us, we have the right, even the responsibility, to say it with the expectation that His power will be released. This vital truth is echoed in Hebrews 13:5-6:

> For he hath said, I will never leave thee, nor forsake thee. So that we may boldly say, The Lord is my helper, and I will not fear what man shall do unto me.

Notice that the boldness of the latter statement is based on the truth of the first one. Since God has said, we may boldly say. Though the second statement is not identical to the first, it is based entirely on it. This leaves an open field of powerful declarations that should grace our lips as we hear what God says and speak out accordingly. I call this the God-has-said-so-I-may-boldly-say principle.

Both the Old and New Testaments are replete with reports of such workings according to the Word of God. In fact, every miracle performed by Jesus was performed by this God-kind of faith in which God's Word was spoken and God's power was released. What an adventure to read the New Testament again and behold the living Word in action against demons, deformity, disease, weather, and rebellion. And the Word prevailed again and again!

*There is infinitely more
to the ministry of the Word than
quoting it, explaining it, and memorizing it.
Having existence with power
in and of itself by the Spirit of God, it can be expected
that the greatest ministry will occur when the human
instrument makes the presentation.
The ministry of the Word follows upon the ministry of
the minister.*

—JRT

Chapter 12

The Minister and Ministry of the Word

The Word of God being what it is makes the ministry of the one who shares the Word significant indeed. If the Word of God was nothing more than information to be mentally processed, expressed, and humanly understood, the nature of the vessel through which it is given would not be so important. But because the Word is alive and full of power, the channel through which it comes is of extreme importance. If it was only a matter of the knowledge of the original languages, word study, and the occasions for the writing of the various parts, the minister of the Word would need only be concerned about the technical knowledge necessary. But because the Word of God is a life form—a power source—the nature of the minister is crucial to the ministry of the Word.

Until recently I was under the impression that the term "the ministry of the Word" simply referred to the teaching or sharing of it. I have come to see that the sharing of the Word is the ministry of the minister of the Word. The ministry of the Word itself is something else. If the minister of the Word is a proper vessel, the ministry of the Word may begin when the minister is ministering but will continue far beyond the time-space dimensions of the specific situation.

The ministry of the Word is something apart from the minister of the Word. Watchman Nee correctly declares that the minister of the Word must be in a right state before God if the Word is to be proclaimed, because any improper condition will automatically corrupt the Word of God. That being true, it is possible to preach the Bible in a technical manner and not preach the Word of God in the strictest sense. The Word of God is still spirit and life and must come through spiritual ministers or it will not have life.

The Word of God has come to us through man and continues to be shared through us today. The person through whom the Word comes must allow the Word to flow through him or her in an unhindered and powerful manner, or the Word will be diluted, hindered, and corrupted by the spiritual condition of the minister. Ministering the Word is a serious matter indeed. The way of God has always been "holy men of God spake as they were moved by the Holy Ghost" (2 Pet. 1:21).

For real ministry to take place, the life of God, the Holy Spirit, must abide in the minister, as well as in the Word. The resurrected Word must be shared by resurrected ministers. If the minister is dead, then the Word he seeks to preach will be stripped of its life. It will be limited, diluted, and powerless. God could speak alone, but he seldom does. His chosen way is to have a minister through whom He speaks. If He can find one He will speak; if not, He will likely not speak. There may be rare exceptions (consider Baalam's donkey!).

The Minister of the Word

Since the Word of God is alive by the same Holy Spirit who first breathed it, only a Holy Spirit-anointed minister can retain its life. If the living Word is to be productive, the one who ministers it must be both illumined by and filled with spiritual life.

The problem has never been in the Word itself but in the minister. The light and life that are in the Scriptures are often dimmed and weakened by the vessel sharing them. A lack of brokenness, the presence of mixed motives, self-seeking, and a plethora of other problems keep the Word from being released in its power. Unless the minister be broken, self will dilute the pure Word of God and steal its power. The minister must be purified until the shining of the Word of God is as bright coming through him or her as it was through Jesus Christ Himself. Then the ministry of the man or woman of God who shares the Word will merely deliver the Word, allowing it to have its matchless ministry. When the Spirit of God connects the minister of the Word with the Word, life flows from that connection.

We have much preaching today but so little ministering of the Word in power. Rhetoric may impress the flesh, but power will bring about a revolution. May we learn to allow the Word to move through us without hindrance. This process can be rather clearly traced in studying the lives of people who have effectively ministered the Word.

First, they were prepared vessels. Paul was a carefully chosen and prepared vessel. Mary's preparation did not begin when Gabriel spoke to her in Luke 1. God had been preparing her beforehand. No minister is given a text and told to begin preaching without inward as well as outward preparation. Through the years it seems that more and more emphasis has been given to outward preparation and less and less emphasis to the inward preparation. An intellectual knowledge of the Scriptures, technical expertise on the art of communication, and skills in psychological manipulation may bring results, but there will be little or no fruit. Fruit is organic, the result of laws of life; results may be organizational, the result of good administration or even manipulation.

Brokenness, humility, selflessness, and singular passion to know Christ and make Him known will bring about fruit in the kingdom. Preaching the Bible with oratorical skill without the Spirit of power may impress the crowds, but there will be no life apart from the Spirit.

It is mandatory that we return to the interior preparation of the one who is to minister the Word. Cleverness and eloquence alone will not do. The ability to conjugate the verbs, parse the nouns, and diagram the sentences may help in understanding what the Scriptures are saying, but unless the vessel is properly prepared, the resulting words will be like clanging pots and off-key trumpets.

Second, they were able to hear the Word of God. Paul was ever itimating, "What I received from God I am sharing with you." The one distinguishing characteristic of all those who have shaped the Christian world is that they were able to hear from God for their age. When Solomon was confronted with that memorable dream at Gibeon, he was faced with a shocking choice. God said in the dream, "Ask for whatever you want me to give you" (1 Kings 3:5, NIV). I have no idea how much time elapsed before Solomon gave his answer, but I imagine that it was a heart-wrenching experience. Most of us would have no trouble making a choice of a dozen things, but one thing is different—what Solomon asked for: a heart that could hear from God. "Give therefore thy servant an understanding [i.e., 'hearing'] heart . . . that I may discern between good and bad" (1 Kings 3:9).

That request so pleased the Lord that He granted Solomon all else that he might have requested. He could have asked for riches, or long life for himself, or victory over his enemies. Instead he asked for the ability to hear the voice of God. God answered this request and gave him such wisdom and understanding that there had been none his equal before him and none after him. And because he made the right request, God granted him riches and honor with the promise of long life if he walked in the ways of God. Though it was a dream, it soon became reality. As long as Solomon listened to God, his greatness was incomparable. When his ears became insensitive to the voice of God, his decline began.

Only through intimacy with God can we know His mind, hear His voice, and move toward His destiny for us and our world. God, give us folks like the sons of Issachar, who had "understanding of the times, to know what Israel ought to do" (1 Chron. 12:32).

Third, they discerned how and when to share the Word. The Word must have time to soak in the spirit until all of it has applied to the one who will minister it. Then, when the burden comes, he is to share it properly and powerfully. Like the alabaster box of ointment was broken by Mary to pour the precious salve upon the head of Jesus, the minister of the Word is broken to release the life-giving Word to the world.

The Ministry of the Word

Here we refer to the work of the Word once it has been shared. We have already observed that the Word of God becomes, when spoken, a life form and an energy source. God sent His Word and healed people through it. He declared that His Word would not return void but would accomplish His desires and will. The Word, once delivered through a prepared vessel, begins its mighty work.

The ministry of the Word is described in a number of ways in the Bible. In Jeremiah God declares that His Word is like a fire and a hammer. Fire destroys, consumes, illumines, and purifies (Jer. 23:29).

The psalmist identifies the Word as a lamp to his feet and a light to his path. It not only ministers light to the feet of the person going but to his path as well (Ps. 119:105).

James declares that the engrafted Word is able to save the soul. This surely refers to more than the salvation experience. It is the ongoing process by which the mighty Word of God purifies and refines the soul (Jas. 1:21).

Paul described the Word as effectually working in those that believed (1 Thess. 2:13).

David recognized that the entrance of the Word brought light (Ps. 119:130).

Peter was keenly aware that the Word of God was the means by which we have been born again: "Being born again, not of corruptible seed, but of incorruptible, by the word of God, which liveth and abideth for ever" (1 Pet. 1:23).

James revealed the same awareness when he declared, "Of his own will begat he us with the word of truth, that we should be a kind of firstfruits of his creatures" (Jas. 1:18).

The Process of the Minister, the Ministry, and the Word

There must first be *revelation* (or illumination if you prefer). Many astute scholars believe that revelation ended with the completion of the canon of Scripture. While I agree that there will be no additions to the text of Scripture, I am deeply convicted that God still illumines.

We must receive light. That light must be more than intellectual understanding. We cannot be saved without light. We will not grow

without light. We cannot minister the Word without light. The secret of the Christian religion is found in these words:

> In him was life; and the life was the light of men.
> And the light shineth in darkness;
> and the darkness comprehended it not. . .
> That was the true Light,
> which lighteth every man that cometh into the world.
> —John 1:4-5,9

Faith requires light. If there is no light, there is no faith. If we are to
walk in and by the Word we must receive the light of the Word. We
must hear the inner voice of God attesting to and confirming what
He has said in the Scriptures. Commentaries may aid in understanding the word meanings, but only God gives light. Knowledge
of Hebrew and Greek is of great value, but it cannot bring light.

His life is the light of man (John 1:4). There is no light apart
from His life. We should always be praying the prayer of Paul for
ourselves and each other:

> That the God of our Lord Jesus Christ,
> the Father of glory, may give unto you the spirit of wisdom
> and revelation in the knowledge of him:
> The eyes of your understanding being enlightened;
> that ye may know.
> —Ephesians 1:17-18

Following the revelation or enlightenment there is the *assimilation.*
The light may come in a single word or verse in the Scripture. It
may begin with a thought. Sometimes it comes in the midst of a
problem, pressures, or crises. What happens after this is dependent
upon the nature of the person receiving it. Spiritual light cannot be
humanly discerned, so attempts to submit it to human logic will be
the death of the revelation. In the process of assimilation the slightest intrusion of our human thinking may soil it. Since the Spirit of
God initiated the light, He must be depended upon to bring more
light. "In thy light shall we see light" (Ps. 36:9).

Vital to the assimilation of light is the bringing of our minds into
accord with His mind. God has made clear that His thoughts are
not our thoughts and His ways not our ways. His thoughts and
ways are as high above ours as the heavens are higher than the
earth (Isa. 55:8-9). This truth should not cause despair in us but
arouse our determination to raise our thoughts to the level of His.

Some time ago I prayed a prayer which went something like this: "God, I want You to change my mind on every issue on which You and I do not now see eye to eye." God has been answering that prayer slowly and, much of the time, painfully. This is a part of the assimilation of light received from God.

Coming to God's thoughts and ways never precludes the use of our minds. This is a mystery beyond explanation. Man receives light; around that light gather words, human words that are familiar to the person receiving light. The light is from God, but the words of the person are his words. So we have God's Word and our words which gather around His Word. When we write them or share them, they have the marks of our personality, the style of our speaking or writing, but, if our hearts are pure, we may deliver the Word of God. What an unfathomable mystery! God puts His Word in us. Our thoughts and words gather around His Word and there is light! They are His words and our words, and they bring light.

It is a perilous experience to receive light from God. It may be received properly and assimilated improperly. It may be both received and assimilated properly and shared improperly. In both instances the result is distortion of truth, heresy, and destruction. This should motivate those who teach the Word of God to strive for purity and take care in the process of ministering the Word.

Another issue of prime importance in this process is that of personal *implementation*. Though actually a part of the assimilation process, it deserves to be treated alone. Some light is for the individual alone. All light must be assumed to apply to the individual receiving it. We must not consider sharing what light we have received until it has been applied fully to our lives.

James gives us some wonderful counsel in the process of experiencing the Word of God:

Be ye doers of the word, and not hearers only, deceiving your own selves. For if any be a hearer of the word, and not a doer, he is like unto a man beholding his natural face in a glass: for he beholdeth himself, and goeth his way, and straightway forgetteth what manner of man he was. But whoso looketh into the perfect law of liberty, and continueth therein, he being not a forgetful hearer, but a doer of the work, this man shall be blessed in his deed.

—James 1:22-25

Implementation of the Word of God means total obedience on the part of the hearer. To seek to minister the Word without implicit obedience is to invite disaster. Jesus said, "Blessed rather are those who hear the word of God and obey it" (Luke 11:28, NIV).

The Pharisees were typical examples of those who had received truth and failed to assimilate it. "Ye have not his word abiding in you: for whom he hath sent, ye believe not . . . Search the scriptures which testify of me" (John 5:38-39). He further accused them of nullifying "the word of God by your tradition that you have handed down" (Mark 7:13, NIV). The word for "nullify" literally means to "strip of authority or lordship."

More than once Jesus warned them to be careful how they heard. He cautioned, "With the measure you use, it will be measured to you—and even more. Whoever has will be given more; whoever does not have, even what he has will be taken from him" (Mark 4:24-25, NIV). In summary, if we do not implement the Word of God we have heard, we will lose it. The received Word must conquer us if its authority is to be retained when we share it.

If the Word is for personal consumption alone, the only burden will be that of completing obedience to it. When that is completed there will be light for the path. "The entrance of thy words giveth light; it giveth understanding unto the simple" (Ps. 119:130).

If the Word received is for wider consumption, as it usually is, a part of the continuing process will be an urge to share. Jeremiah identified this urge as "like a fire [in his heart], a fire shut up in my bones" (Jer. 20:9, NIV). God had told him previously, "I will make my words in your mouth a fire" (Jer. 5:14).

After the Word has done its first work in us, namely sorting out and burning up the trash in the minister, we may then be concerned about the timing and manner of our sharing it. This is always preceded by a process of sensitizing which causes discomfort. A Word from God which must be shared may cause great inner disturbance and can be identified as a "burden." This is the fire that God promised and Jeremiah experienced. He could not keep the Word in himself. It was a fire burning for an outward expression.

So to the process involving illumination, assimilation, and implementation, we add *expediency* or *burden*. The word used in this sense means "a message to be shared."

This expediency to share is spoken of by several of the prophets:

Isaiah 13:1 The burden of Babylon . . .

Isaiah 15:1 The burden of Moab.

Isaiah 17:1 The burden of Damascus.

Isaiah 19:1 The burden of Egypt.

Isaiah 21:1 The burden of the desert of the sea.

Isaiah 23:1 The burden of Tyre.

Jeremiah 23:33 What is the burden of the LORD?

Nahum 1:1 The burden of Nineveh.

Habakkuk 1:1 The burden which Habakkuk the prophet did see.

Zechariah 9:1; 12:1 The burden of the word of the LORD . . .

In these examples the burden and the message were the same. This burden will be like a fire in our bones, and we will possess a pressing urge to share.

While every stage of the process is important, none is more crucial than the *presentation*. The message will have gone through the processes of illumination, assimilation, and implementation. In the process the vessel or minister is being prepared for the presentation. The message is growing in him like a baby in a mother's womb, taking shape and definition. It is important to be able to discern who, when, where, and how this is to be done.

The Objects—Who?

After determining that the message is to be shared, the object or objects must be discerned. It may be for another person, a family, or a large group, such as a church; perhaps even for a nation. The identification of the recipient or recipients will bring peace.

The Timing—When?

There is a right time for a baby to be born. Likewise, there is a proper time for a message to be delivered. There may be unfortunate consequences if the right message is delivered at the wrong time. A part of the illumination accompanying the message will be the timing. Instructions are contained within it.

The Location—Where?

There will be a place of God's choosing that forms the perfect atmosphere for the sharing of the burden. God will have prepared it much as He did the colt tied in the village destined to be the transportation for Jesus' triumphal entry. The timing of God is always perfect and is as much a part of the revelation as is the message itself. Jesus, being in perfect accord with the Father, was always on time; never in a hurry, His timing was flawless!

The Manner—How?

How shall the message be shared? How will we be able to share a message without our own anger, impatience, or irritation clouding it? The Word itself will have done its work in us. The Holy Spirit will have produced His fruit in us. That fruit is the full-orbed character of Christ. The vessel engages in the presentation of the Word of God. It is earthen so that the "excellency of the power may be of God, and not of us" (2 Cor. 4:7).

Then the Word, having been received by us, ministered in us, and ministered through us will begin its powerful ministry. We may be sure that its success is fully guaranteed!

> Not one of all the LORD's good promises to the house of Israel failed; every one was fulfilled
> —Joshua 21:45, NIV

> There hath not failed one word of all his good promise, which he promised by the hand of Moses his servant.
> —1 Kings 8:56

> So shall my word be that goeth forth out of my mouth: it shall not return unto me void, but it shall accomplish that which I please, and it shall prosper in the thing whereto I sent it.
> —Isaiah 55:11

It will succeed. You have God's Word on it!

Prayer

Father, I give You heartfelt thanks for being chosen to be an agent of Your powerful Word. Prepare my heart to receive and, having received it, enable me to let it have its perfect work in me. Then, at the appointed time, to the appointed people, in the appointed location, in the appointed manner, empower me to share it in Your anointing. For this I live!

AMEN!

و

The only real authority
on the Word of God
is God Himself,
who is its Author.
In the Bible
He has made clear His disposition
what He has said,
is saying,
and will say.
—JRT

Chapter 13

God's Word on God's Word

We have not heard the final word on any word until we have heard the Word of God. When we have God's Word on it, we have the final, authoritative, and ultimate assessment. You and I are what we are because of the fact that we have taken someone's word for everything. We are a composite result of all the words we have received and processed. We have been enjoined in both the Old Testament and New Testament that man is not to live by bread alone but by every word that proceeds out of the mouth of God. Our lives are to be lived, sustained, and regulated by the words of God. What God has to say on any subject is valid. This includes what He says about what He says.

I have personally found it helpful to go through the Bible to find what God has said about His Word or what His Spirit prompted men to say about it. It is deeply reassuring to hear God's Word about His Word. When we encounter God's assessment of His Word we tend to joyfully agree with Him, and with that comes a multitude of accompanying advantages. Some of these references have been identified previously, while others are listed for the first time. The word for "word," referring to what God says, is used in some form more than one thousand times in the Bible, and there are hundreds of other times when it is referred to as "commandments," "statutes," "testimonies," "law," "judgments," or "precepts." I have listed these sayings in separate categories under God, Himself; the Psalmist; Christ; the Early Church; Paul; Peter and others. This will serve for easier reference later. Since most of these are quoted in some part of this volume, I will paraphrase them.

God, Himself, on His Word

Most of the references to the Word of God in the Bible are from men who were touched by the Spirit to say what they said. A few times God Himself spoke. To me, these are of signal significance.

In Isaiah 55:10-11 God illustrates the work of His Word by nature's cycles. The rain and snow come down from heaven, water the earth, and then return. They leave in their wake productivity and blessing. God's Word is the same. It leaves His mouth, becomes a living power, accomplishes its cycle of blessing, and returns to God. No word that has been spoken by God over the universe about anything will fail! His record will remain the same as reported in Joshua 21:45 and 1 Kings 8:56: "Not one of all the LORD'S good promises to the house of Israel failed; every one was fulfilled." and "Not one word has failed of all the good promises he gave through his servant Moses" (NIV).

This is a record that will never be broken.

In Isaiah 66 we see a window into God's deep feelings. The person who will be noticed by God, who will have His esteem, is one who is humble and contrite and trembles at God's Word. It is great to know that the person who takes His Word seriously will have God's esteem!

In Jeremiah 23:29 God gives us two similes that, in His mind, characterize His Word. In verse 28 God commands, "Let the one who has my word speak it faithfully"(NIV). His Word will be like a fire and a hammer which breaks the rock in pieces. History is replete with the records of the work of the Word of God in burning and breaking with its glorious power.

The Psalmist

No author in the Bible seems more aware of the Word of God than the psalmist (or psalmists). The Word of God is referred to in the Psalms under a variety of names, such as judgments, testimonies, precepts, statutes, commandments, law, and ordinances. Some of these references are found in Psalm 19:7-11:

> The law of the Lord is flawless, converting the soul.
>
> The statutes of the Lord are right, making the simple wise.
>
> The precepts of the Lord bring joy to the heart.
>
> The commandment of the Lord is radiant, giving light to the eyes.
>
> The ordinances of the Lord are true and righteous altogether.

The words of God are assessed as more precious than gold, sweeter than honey and the honeycomb, valid warning signals, and rewarding to keep (Ps. 19:10-11).

In Psalm 29 the voice of the Lord is mentioned seven times. His voice has power and majesty to:

> Break the cedars of Lebanon (v. 5).
>
> Divide the flames of fire (v. 7).
>
> Shake the wilderness of Kadesh (v. 8).
>
> Twist the oaks (v. 9).
>
> Strip the forests bare (v. 9).

The psalmist knew something of the power of the Word of God as a creative dynamic. In Psalm 33 he said:

> The word of the Lord is right and true (v. 4).
>
> By the word of the Lord were the heavens made, their starry host by the breath of His mouth (v. 6).
>
> For He spoke and it came to be; He commanded and it stood fast (v. 9).

While mining for the gold of the Word of God in the Psalms, we hit a mother lode in Psalm 119. More than 180 references are given to the Word of God in 176 verses! Here are samples of his concepts of the Word of God:

They are blessed who walk according to His law and keep His statutes (vv. 1-2).

Purity results from living according to the Word (v. 9).

Hiding God's Word in our hearts is a preventative to sin (v. 11).

We should rejoice in following His statutes as one rejoices in great riches (v. 14).

God's Word is a means of preserving life (v. 25).

A weary soul finds strength in the Word (v. 28).

All God's commandments are trustworthy (v. 86).

God's Word is eternal (vv. 89-90).

God's Word is a lamp to the feet and a light to the path (v. 105).

The entering of God's Word gives light (v. 130).

Those who love God's law have great peace and nothing can make them stumble (v. 165).

The highest position of the Word of God is recognized in Psalm 138:2 as the psalmist declared, "For thou hast magnified thy word above all thy name."

There is little doubt that the psalmist had a mature concept of the centrality and power of the Word of God.

Jesus Christ on the Word

References to the Word of God by Christ are quotes from the Old Testament. Among these is the one used against the devil during the temptation. The written Word became alive on His lips and was powerful to defeat the devil. The quote is from Deuteronomy 8:3:

And he humbled thee, and suffered thee to hunger, and fed thee with manna, which thou knewest not, neither did thy fathers know; that he might make thee know that man doth not live by bread only, but by every word that proceedeth out of the mouth of the LORD doth man live.

The Word of God was the subject of the principal parable among all the parables that Jesus gave. This is recorded in Matthew 13,

Mark 4, and Luke 8. It is the parable of the sower, the seed, and the soil. Jesus indicated that it was unlikely that they could understand any parable without an understanding of this one. In explaining the parable Jesus stated, "Now the parable is this: The seed is the Word of God" (Luke 8:11).

In referring to His own words, Jesus stated that they would never pass away (Matt. 24:35; Luke 21:33).

The Pharisees were scored by Jesus for nullifying the Word of God with their traditions (Mark 7:13).

Mary was impregnated by the Word of God (Luke 1:37).

Folks were amazed that Jesus taught the Word of God with power and authority (Luke 4:32).

Demons were removed from people through Jesus' use of words (Luke 4:36).

Miracles resulted when the disciples obeyed the Word of Jesus (Luke 5:5-7).

The centurion understood the concept of the authority of the Word of God as he trusted Jesus to simply "say in a word, and my servant shall be healed" (Luke 7:7).

Jesus pronounced a blessing on those who hear the Word of God and obey it (Luke 11:28).

Eternal life belongs to those who hear His Word and believe in God (John 5:24).

He said of His words, "They are spirit, and they are life" (John 6:63).

Knowing the truth is the means of freedom (John 8:32).

Abiding in Christ and abiding in His words are the prerequisites to continuously answered prayer (John 15:7).

Jesus prayed that God would sanctify us through the truth, truth being identified as "thy Word" (John 17:17).

The Early Church

The Word of God was central in the early church. More than two hundred references to the Word are noted in Acts, with sixty-one more references to the Scripture or Scriptures.

The early church was filled with the Spirit and spoke the Word of God boldly (Acts 4:31).

Four times in Acts the Word of God is reported to have increased (Acts 8:7), to have grown and multiplied (Acts 12:24), to have spread throughout the region (Acts 13:49), and to have mightily grown (Acts 19:20). It is rather certain that the church grew in size and power in accord with the increase of the Word of God in it.

In Acts 17 the Bereans received the Word of God from Paul and immediately examined the Scriptures to see if what he said was true, a response exhibiting nobility of character (v. 11).

The Ephesian elders were challenged by Paul to receive the Word of His grace which could build them up and give them an inheritance among the saints (Acts 20:32).

Paul

He called the gospel (the Word of God) the "power of God unto salvation to every one that believeth" (Rom. 1:16).

He was obligated to preach it, unashamed of it, and found it to reveal the righteousness of God from faith to faith (Rom. 1:14,16,17).

The Word of faith is as close to us as our mouths, and confession of it will bring salvation (Rom. 10:8).

The Word of God is recognized as a means of purification for the church, "cleansing her by the washing with water through the word" (Eph. 5:26, NIV).

The only offensive weapon listed in the believer's battle regalia is the "sword of the Spirit, which is the word of God" (Eph. 6:17).

Paul expressed great gratitude for the response of the Thessalonians' reception of the Word of God which released the Word to work effectually in them (1 Thess. 2:13).

Paul reminded Timothy that everything God created was good and was to be received with thanksgiving, because it was consecrated by the Word of God and prayer (1 Tim. 4:5).

Paul challenged Timothy to present himself to God as one who could correctly handle the Word of truth (2 Tim. 2:15).

A thoroughly equipped man of God will take advantage of the God-breathed (*theopneustos*) Word for every good work (2 Tim. 3:16).

Peter

We are affirmed as having been born again, not of perishable seed, but of imperishable, the living and enduring Word of God which abides forever (1 Pet. 1:23-25).

Peter had been among those who were eyewitnesses of God's majesty. They had heard the voice of God affirming His own Son, saying, "This is my Son, whom I love; with him I am well pleased" (2 Pet. 1:17, NIV). More sure than his report as an eyewitness is the Scripture spoken by holy men as they were carried along by the Holy Spirit (2 Pet. 1:19,21).

Echoing the truths of Genesis and the reflections of the Psalmist, Peter confirms again the power of the Word of God in the creation: "But they deliberately forget that long ago by God's word the heavens existed and earth was formed out of water and by water" (2 Pet. 3:5, NIV).

"By the same word the present heavens and earth are reserved for fire, being kept for the day of judgment and destruction of ungodly men" (2 Pet. 3:7).

Author of Hebrews

It is generally conceded that the author of Hebrews is unknown. Whoever he was, we can be certain that he had a working knowledge of the power of the Word of God.

Jesus, the radiance of God's glory, the perfect representation of His being, sustains all things by His powerful Word (Heb. 1:3).

There is no loftier description of the Word of God to be found anywhere in Scripture than in Hebrews 4:12 (NIV):

> For the word of God is living and active.
> Sharper than any double-edged sword, it penetrates
> even to dividing soul and spirit, joints and marrow;
> it judges the thoughts and attitudes of the heart.

James

The Word of God planted in us is able to save (heal) our souls (Jas. 1:21).

We are to do more than merely listen to what the Word of God says; we are to obey it, which will result in great blessings:

> But the man who looks intently into the perfect law
> that gives freedom, and continues to do this,
> not forgetting what he has heard, but doing it—
> he will be blessed in what he does.
> —James 1:25, NIV

First John

The Word of Life is the subject of 1 John. John is echoing what he has heard from Him who is the Word of Life. We have observed that the Word was a person before it was anything else. The first verses of 1 John leave no doubt as to the identity of the subject:

"That which was from the beginning, which we have heard, which we have seen with our eyes, which we have looked upon and our hands have handled, of the Word of Life" (1 John 1:1).

Out of Him who was and is the Word of life flows a message:

This then is the message which we have heard of him, and declare unto you, that God is light, and in him is no darkness at all. If we say that we have fellowship with him, and walk in darkness, we lie, and do not the truth. But if we walk in the light, as he is in the light, we have fellowship one with another, and the blood of Jesus Christ his Son cleanseth us from all sin. If we say that we have not sinned, we make him a liar, and his word is not in us.

—1 John 1:5-7,10.

John addressed young men who were strong and had the Word of God living in them (1 John 2:14).

It is obvious from these references which make up only a part of the whole that the words of the Bible on the Word of God are in agreement with the greatness of its power. The Word of God has pervaded the universe and holds all things together by its power. Nothing that was created was created without the Word of God and nothing in creation now is unrelated to the Word. That Word of God is working in His world to bring the whole cosmos to its destiny.

So we have what God has said about His Word and what He has breathed upon others to say as recorded in the Scriptures. On no subject is the Bible more integrated and uniform than on the identity, nature, and power of the Word.

ॐ

*It is not likely
that we can get to where we desire to be
until we find out where we are.
Any crisis is lessened by an understanding
of how we and it fit together.
The Bible is not only a proper map
but a locator of where we are on the map.*

—JRT

Chapter 14

The Word That Shakes the World

See that ye refuse not him that speaketh. For if they escaped not who refused him that spake on earth, much more shall not we escape, if we turn away from him that speaketh from heaven: Whose voice then shook the earth: but now he hath promised, saying, Yet once more I shake not the earth only, but also heaven. And this word, Yet once more, signifieth the removing of those things that are shaken, as of things that are made, that those things which cannot be shaken may remain. Wherefore we receiving a kingdom which cannot be moved, let us have grace, whereby we may serve God acceptably with reverence and godly fear: For our God is a consuming fire.

—Hebrews 12:25-29

Several years ago a song hit the charts entitled "A Whole Lot of Shakin' Goin' On." It is not likely to win a place with the great music of the ages, but it carried a message that is without argument.

Finding Out Where We Are

I am a people-watcher. I would rather watch people than go to a zoo. Though shopping is not high on my list of things to do, I love to go to shopping malls just to watch people. Some years ago I had a free day between engagements and was lodged in a hotel right across from a gigantic shopping mall. I walked across the street, entered one of the mall's many entrances, and paused before a directory which indicated the locations of the stores by color and number. I quickly discovered a basic principle of life: I could not get where I wanted to go until I found out where I was! The directory and map before me formed a meaningless maze of colors, lines, and numbers. I might have learned from the directory what stores were there and where they were in relation to each other, but I had not a clue where I was relative to where they were.

Suddenly I was saved from my bewilderment by a little red dot at the lower left-hand corner, accompanied by the words, "YOU ARE HERE!" It was amazing how clear the directory and map became!

The world today is a maze of color, numbers, and lines. Add to this confusing scene a thousand voices saying, "This is the way; walk in it!" The ceaseless cacophony distracts us and fatigues us. We know that we are on a journey and are aware at times where we want to go, but we wonder, all the while, "Where are we?" Somebody needs to step forward and paint a little red dot on the confusing landscape to mark: "YOU ARE HERE!"

This is precisely the purpose of the passage that begins this chapter! It seems to suggest to our chaotic and confused culture, "It is not likely that you are going to get where you want to be if you cannot figure out where you are. It is time to look and listen. You are here, and this is what is happening!"

We live in a changing culture. Everything is speeding up, except perhaps the mail. New technologies are coming into effect every day. The life span of these new technologies is now less than two years. Much of the knowledge acquired today will be obsolete the day after tomorrow.

Conventional wisdom is being called into serious question and, in many cases, is failing the interrogation. Business is recognizing the threat of this rapidly changing age to be valid, "Revise or die!" That message is underlined by the sight of businesses which, a few months ago, were at the top of the corporate ladder in production and profits but now are dinosaurs fighting for their lives.

Every now and again someone sounds a message that grabs the attention of the business world. Its approach is forward and bold. Such a book is *If It Ain't Broke, Break It!* I was recently walking through the airport and noticed this book with its daring message glaring at me through the rushing crowd. What struck me about it was that the title suggested something that God could have written. He seems to be specializing in the breaking business these days. Well, I plunked down more than twenty dollars to buy this book only to discover, as I read it, that what is happening in the business world is the same thing that is happening in the church. Things, "they are a-changin'!" Accepted rules are being debunked. Old things are passing away. Anger, confusion, and strife are resulting.

The final decade of the twentieth century will see more changes than the ninety years that went before them. It doesn't take a genius to discover that if we are going to survive we must link ourselves to something that is known for stability.

Back to Hebrews 12! Here is a word from God. We not only have an accurate map for the journey, the Bible; we have an unerring Guide, the Holy Spirit in us. Let's examine this passage.

The Shaker

Who is responsible for the turbulence of the age? Who is presiding over the rise and fall of the nations? Whose hand is carving such changes on the landscape of the planet? The answer to this question is all-important. Our passage strongly assumes the answer.

"See that ye refuse not him that speaketh"(Heb. 12:25). Somebody is talking, and the world would do well to listen.

We are reminded that God's voice once shook the earth and those who did not heed the voice did not escape. The reference is shrouded in mystery, "If they escaped not who refused him that spake on earth"(v. 25). It may be a reference to Christ as He walked the earth speaking on God's behalf. It may be referring to the God who spoke in thunder, fire, and smoke from the mountain where

Moses was. Regardless, the message is patently clear: God is speaking and we had better listen!

The quote suggests a passage in Haggai 2:6-7:

> For thus saith the LORD of hosts;
> Yet once, it is a little while, and I will shake the heavens,
> and the earth, and the sea, and the dry land;
> and I will shake all nations,
> and the desire of all nations shall come:
> and I will fill this house with glory,
> saith the LORD of hosts.

The issue of the shaking is a Word issue. The power behind the world shaking is none other than the Word of our God. His voice is shaking the earth. You may ask, "How can a voice shake the earth?" Don't ever forget that it was the voice of God that created the world and the whole created universe. His voice authored all that is—every cell, every atom, every molecule, every galaxy. His voice, His spoken and speaking Word, holds sway in this universe.

The voice that had the power to shape the worlds also has the power to shake the worlds! And that is what is happening. He who spoke is still speaking, and His Word is still shaping and shaking the worlds. He will be heard.

While the manner of this shaking is vocal, a message, a word, the measure of this shaking is to the extent of the earth and heavens. "I shake not the earth only, but also heaven"(Heb. 12:26).

This is no time to worry about eschatological mysteries. Is this the terminal generation? Will Jesus come back to earth in my lifetime? How near or far are we from the end? Where does America fit into the last days? What about Israel? Iran? Iraq? Germany? Russia (what's left of it!)? What about the Antichrist?

Read my lips: I D-O-N'-T K-N-O-W! And neither do you. The sooner we quit trying to find out what God has deemed to be none of our business the sooner we will get up to the right business. The important thing is that somebody is saying something, and that Somebody is God, and that something is the same eternal truth of which the worlds are made, the Word of God!

Lesser players are grabbing the headlines, but behind the scene is our all-powerful God. William L. Stidger may have little realized the prophetic tone of his verse:

History's pages but record
One death grapple in the darkness
'Twixt old systems and the Word;
Right forever on the scaffold,
Wrong forever on the throne.
But that scaffold sways the future,
And beyond the dim unknown . . .
Standeth God within the shadows,
Keeping watch above His own!

The turbulence in some regions of the world may seem to have been initiated by a provincial personality or by some emerging leader previously unknown. The shaking may be credited to a collection of political phenomena. It must be kept in mind, however, that the shaker is God. He is behind it all! Many personalities on the scene are morally and spiritually incorrigible, but they are not center stage. That position is still held by God! The God who puts the kings and leaders in place can quickly put any one of them in his place—out!

We need to repeat it until we believe it: GOD is in charge! Lesser lights are shining and are being seen. Lesser voices are sounding off and are being heard. But know for sure that it is God behind this speaking and shaking!

A clear example of this fact is in the story of Joseph in the last chapters of Genesis. Joseph, his father's favorite, did not win any popularity contests with his brothers. When he told them of his dreams in which they were subject to him, their hate and envy became more intense. His brothers planned to kill him and tell his father that he had died a victim of a wild animal.

At the last minute they changed their plans and sold him wholesale to some traveling merchants from Egypt.

The story continues over a period of more than twenty years. Joseph was subjected to one injustice after another. He was falsely accused and sent to prison. Wherever Joseph found himself, however, he acted in such a manner as to achieve promotion and favor. In a short time he was in charge of all the prisoners in the jail because "the Lord was with Joseph, and shewed him mercy, and gave him favor in the sight of the keeper of the prison" (Gen. 39:21).

There was a glimmer of hope when Joseph interpreted the dreams of the butler and the baker. One would die, the other live.

The baker died; the butler lived and was restored to his position in service to the king. The butler forgot about Joseph, however, until Pharaoh dreamed a dream the interpretation of which was beyond the abilities of his wise men and magicians. Then the butler remembered Joseph and told Pharaoh about his ability to interpret dreams. Joseph was called upon to exercise his remarkable ability. Joseph's response was, "It is not in me: God shall give Pharaoh an answer of peace" (Gen. 41:16). The dreams were about a coming time of plenty followed by a time of famine. God gave Joseph the whole plan of survival for the nation. He was quickly appointed second-in-command. His promotion from prison cell to vice-president in one day is without precedent!

The seven years of plenty came and went, but tons of food were laid up in every city because of the dual words of knowledge and wisdom God gave Joseph. He had not only told the king what was in the mind of God; he told him what the nation should do about it.

Then came the years of crushing famine. As the people began to be hungry, they came to Pharaoh, who sent them to Joseph. Not only was Egypt cared for, but all the surrounding countries as well, including the land of Canaan, Joseph's home country. Sure enough, twenty years after they had sold their brother into Egypt, Joseph's brothers were bowing before him, pleading with him to sell them food! Not until much later and after many episodes did Joseph reveal to them his identity. When he, weeping, told them who he was, they were troubled.

I have shared this well-known story to underline this vital point: it is God beyond the lesser actors in your drama who is controlling your situation, and it is God behind the headlines who is running this show. Joseph said two things to his brothers:

First, he told them, "It was not you . . . but God" (Gen. 45:8).

Second, he said, "Ye thought evil against me; but God meant it unto good" (Gen. 50:20).

If you will cling to these two statements as you face the approaching storms of shakings, the time it took to tell this oft-told story will prove worthwhile indeed. Say it with me:

"It isn't they . . . It's God!"

"They intend evil but God means to do good!"

God, and God alone, is the Shaker!

The Shaking

We have identified the Shaker; let us briefly observe the shaking. It takes the form of a message and will extend to the earth and heavens. All that can be shaken will be shaken until all that remains will be that which is unshakable. All created things are shakable, impermanent. These brief verses describe not only the nature of the shaking and the extent of the shaking, but the timing of the shaking: "That those things which cannot be shaken may remain"(Heb. 12:27). The shaking will not stop until everything that is shakable is removed. Everything! We will witness a shaking in the social, political, medical, economic, educational, and religious world. It will touch the corporate as well as the personal dimensions of our lives. No amount of pleading will save the superficial systems of this world order! They are bound for destruction, marked for extinction.

Do not, I repeat, do not decry the shaking! It is both inevitable and necessary. It is a bad-news-good-news situation. The bad news is that there will be a whole lot of discomfort involved for us all; the good news is that behind it and beyond it is the goodness of God who will bring us to His highest purposes. The purpose of this shaking is twofold: one, to expose that which is not worthy of our trust; and, two, to exalt that which is worthy. Thus God must shake the world until the false is exposed and the real is exalted.

The Shaken

We have looked at the Shaker and have examined the shaking; now, let us observe the shaken, you and me. It is vital that we know the acceptable protocol for the days of the shaking. The passage makes this very clear.

We are to listen to the voice. "See that ye refuse not him that speaketh" (v. 25). You can hear if you will listen.

A layman friend was sharing his testimony with me about this matter of hearing from God. He shared how he had often complained to God that he could not hear Him. One day God brought him up short with the sudden thought, "If you would stop saying that you cannot hear Me, you could hear Me!" That did it for him, and to his pleasant consternation he began to hear from God.

As long as we are saying we cannot hear from God, we will not hear from God. It is logistically, biologically, and scientifically impossible to hear anything clearly while we are talking. The secret to hearing God is listening!

We are to receive a kingdom. "Wherefore we receiving a kingdom which cannot be moved"(v. 28). If we are to achieve permanence in these changing times we must link ourselves to something that is going to last. Noah and his family survived the flood by getting into something that was built to survive floods, the ark. Nothing in our society was built with this kind of shaking in mind. All the kingdoms of man will fall—all of them. What does it mean to receive a kingdom? There are three things involved in a kingdom:

> ➤ There is a ruler.
> ➤ There are the ruled.
> ➤ There are the rules.

To receive the kingdom, we must acknowledge the Ruler, admit to being the ruled, and accede to the rules. This procedure will serve to prepare us for the shaking.

We are to have grace. Our attitude is to be one of favor toward God and man. The *New International Version* translates it, "Let us be thankful"(v. 28). Praise God for the shaking. Complaining may serve to lengthen and intensify the process.

The worse things get, the better things get! It is going to get so bad that all of us will get to trust God! Hallelujah!

We are to worship God. It seems a truism that in good times church worship attendance becomes poor. We turn to worshipping what consumes us and that which provides for us. In these days we have learned to trust the government, the doctors, the educators, the insurance companies, and whatever and whoever else has provided our high standard of living. But the spigots are running dry. The voices of the experts are dying out on the howling winds of change. The storehouses are almost depleted.

In these times we will shout for joy when our team wins—at anything! But we are self-conscious about putting any effort into worshipping God with any degree of excitement. I predict that out of this present crisis will come a pure worship heretofore unknown in recent centuries.

"Let us have grace, whereby we may serve [worship] God acceptably with reverence and godly fear" (Heb. 12:28).

The word used here for service is *latreuo*, which has to do with worship, as over against *diakomis*, which has to do with serving by doing things. We must first serve in worship before we can effectively serve through service. God wants our worship first, then our service.

This passage does not end quietly.

"For our God is a consuming fire!"

What a finale! The twentieth-century Christian in the Western world is not well acquainted with this side of God.

Fire consumes. God is the ultimate consuming fire. His fire will burn up all that is combustible. Do you remember His words in the days of Jeremiah?

"IS NOT MY WORD LIKE AS A FIRE (Jer. 23:29)?"

That burning Word is going forth. I am told that a raging fire will create its own storms. It is happening!

Fire purifies. When fire comes, all that is combustible vanishes in ashes. Fire is used to refine gold; the hotter the fire, the purer the gold.

Fire enlightens. While it consumes and purifies, it also reveals the issues heretofore undetected in darkness.

The Word of God with power is shaking the world! The Shaker is God! The nature of the shaking is clear. We, the shaken, may settle on the unshakable kingdom and be safe.

ॐ

Prepare for change—
dramatic and sometimes painful change!
Change for the sake of change
may land us in a worse state than at present.
A proper understanding
of the Spirit and the Word
will facilitate proper change.
—JRT

Chapter 15

So—What Now?

If the church comes to believe that God is still speaking and we should be listening, what are the implications in Christianity as we face the twenty-first century? What are the implications for individual Christians? for local churches? for parachurch organizations? for the whole of Christianity?

That there will be drastic changes in the entire Christian landscape is a foregone conclusion. The church of the twenty-first century will surely have a new face as well as a new body. It will be unique both in its public expression and in its inner structure. No one knows how unique this new phenomenon will be, but it would seem wise at least to anticipate some of its features for advantages in preparation.

Individual Implications

Centrality of Relationships

A more relationship-oriented Christianity is very likely to emerge. If the real purpose of the Bible is to initiate and implement a personal relationship with the living God, one vital result of this emphasis on the Word of God with power will doubtlessly be a fresh excitement and emphasis on relationships in general. Bible knowledge for Bible knowledge's sake fails to be fulfilling and satisfying in the long run. Lonely, modern folks are looking for the warmth of relationships. Individual believers in the church today are falling through the cracks and getting lost in megamemberships and dropping out in large numbers. They are weary of being a part of impressive statistics in a corporate sense while being disregarded generally in a personal sense. A recent response typifies this feeling! "I am tired of being a non-person in the church; I feel like a figure, a thing to be used to accomplish a goal." As God's contemporary personhood is reflected in His children hearing from Him personally and relating to Him dynamically, a normal sequence will be the development of dynamic relationships between believers.

The Priesthood of the Believer

While a basic tenet of evangelical Christianity, the concept of the priesthood of the believer has taken a diminishing role in emphases on church growth while celebrity leadership takes center stage. At the center of most church growth strategies, despite rhetoric to the contrary, is, in most cases, a strong, determined, and winsome personality around whom folks gather who want to be with, under, and around a hero. This leader-with-everything-together knows Hebrew and Greek, speaks with eloquence, administers with authority and definition, and charms the old and young with equal ease. This condition is one major reason why the Christian world is so ripe for cult leaders. This is about to change and the change will be radical.

The priesthood of the believer is back! Common folk are finding out they can hear God's voice through Bible truth, their theological ignorance notwithstanding. It should be realistically expected that at times this will be messy. There will be people thinking they are hearing from God, when, in reality, they are expressing their own opinions. Flaky folk will abound. The enemy will surely seek to seize the opportunity and plant charlatans among God's sheep. This will necessitate a heightened discernment among the people of God, as well as structures which provide checks and balances. The open church where all are priests will demand a call for order and protection against confusion. Today's church with its rather closed agenda has not had to be greatly concerned about unplanned intrusions.

Before we choose against the risk factor we should keep in mind that factories, where production is in progress, are high risks for messes. This is a part of progress. The easiest place to keep order is the cemetery. All its occupants are settled. They offer no arguments. They engage in no intrusions. Such is not the case where there are living, responsible people in a growth mode.

Rethinking of Leadership

The one-man show may be over. The concept of the pastor as hired man, designated hitter, and surrogate servant for the whole congregation will diminish in favor of the pastor-as-equipper concept. If indeed the individual is given dignity as one who hears from God and whose resources are as valuable as anyone's, that individual should be equipped and released. The seemingly advantageous idea of the pastor as corporate executive officer carries with it painful and costly side effects. Among them is the feeling on the part of the stockholders (church members) that they can criticize him at will and relieve him of responsibility in the event of diminished productivity.

It may be painful to high profile leaders at first to sense that their celebrity status is diminishing, but it will be obviously profitable in the long run. Men of God, taxed to the limit with congregational demands, stressed to the breaking point by production quotas, and performing as magicians and jugglers with a myriad of dates, projects, and expectations, can relax a bit while the laity happily shares the load.

A Fresh Excitement over the Bible

While it may be feared that the emphasis of this book may depreciate the value of the glorious Book, the Bible, to some believers, I believe that the opposite will prove true. It has been so for me.

While Bible study, of itself, is of great value, it often occurs without the student getting beyond the cognitive or logical understanding of its truths. When the student recognizes that what God has said He is still saying, the study of the Scriptures will mean the experiencing of the inner voice of God. Likewise, as the Spirit breathes afresh upon the written Word, it becomes a dynamic expression of and an encounter with the living God.

The Bible is wonderful, but with all its wonder, it is still just the menu; the meal is the living Lord. This realization came rather suddenly one day as I began to explain what I was discovering about the Word of God with power. I had talked to this young man only a few moments when he exclaimed, "Well, my goodness, we have mistaken the menu for the meal." My thoughts have gone back to that statement again and again during the past months. With each review I am more convinced that he was imminently correct. The menu (the Bible) is replete with all the delicious foods the human soul will ever need. The descriptions are not wanting but are thorough and inviting. We have majored on explaining, interpreting, and presenting the menu. We have even learned to discuss it alliteratively and expositorily, with points and subpoints taken from the text. We have translated it and retranslated it, seeking to refine our understanding of it through the varying shades of meaning reflected in the original languages of Hebrew and Greek.

We have built institutions and offered specialized studies for those who sense a call to full-time professions of explaining the menu. The ones who can present the menu with greatest oratory and appeal are rewarded with the larger "restaurants." We have made it a fine art and have greatly emphasized the ability to engage in the art form of preaching. But if we are not careful we will major on the menu (the Bible) to the exclusion of the meal (the living Word). Our folks will go away full—full of study, oratory, and art—but go away empty without the Bread of Life.

The Pharisees made the mistake of choosing the Scriptures over Jesus Himself. Jesus denounced them by saying, "Ye have not his word abiding in you: for whom he hath sent, him ye believe not. Search the Scriptures; for in them ye think ye have eternal life: and they are they which testify of me" (John 5:38-39). It is great to be excited about and devoted to the written Word but greater should be the intrigue and devotion to the Person of the living Word, the

Lord Jesus Christ. I candidly confess to you that I am more impressed with the wonder and truthfulness of the Bible as God's Word than I have ever been.

Pneumaphobia Will Be Cured

When we speak of someone who has died we tend to say, "This is what he or she said." When we refer to someone living we say, "This is what he or she is saying." What a difference! In the first case the words are old and still; in the second, they are living and active. God is alive—neither still nor silent. What He has said, He is still saying. If He is speaking, He is surely active in His world. He remains the great I AM and if He is, then neither His speaking nor His activity is diminished. When this is realized, this on-site, here-and-now, present-tense, contemporary God will be the subject of conversation and the object of adoration.

Who is He? Jesus identified Him as the Paraclete, the "one called alongside," the Holy Spirit. In this church of the twenty-first century the Holy Spirit will surely have His proper office space to do His office work. Faith in Him will cause fear of Him to vanish. He will come in freshness and power, brooding over the chaos of man's organizations and the darkness of man's ignorance. He will speak light to the scene and once again He will breathe His power and life into the almost comatose body of Christ on earth, the church.

Spurgeon was right when he said,

> We might preach until our tongues rotted or till we should exhaust our tongues and die, but never a soul would be converted unless there was a mysterious power going with it, the Holy Spirit, changing the wills of men. We may as well preach to stone walls as to humanity unless the Holy Spirit be with the Word to give it power to convert the soul.

We must be ready to answer the question, "By what power have you done this?" with the reply, "Not by our might, or our power but by His Spirit!"

Surely in the church of tomorrow the blessed third Person of the Trinity will have a central place from which to share His fruit, His gifts, His guidance, His light, and His power. So might it be!

The first twenty-five years of my Christian life and ministry were greatly restricted by a fear of the Holy Spirit (pneumaphobia) because of unfortunate associations in my youth. Praise the Lord for the end of that era in my life through the present power of the Word of God.

Implications for the Church

An Open Agenda?

There are few justifications in Scripture for church as it is held today. Seldom, if ever, in Scripture do we hear of a gathering with an appointed speaker and a designated program in a planned setting. Most of the gatherings were spontaneous; the program was unplanned; and the speaker happened (providentially!) to be there. The meetings often were dialogues with questions and answers and many times were punctuated with welcomed intrusions. There were times when the meetings featured a planned debate by Jesus' opposition that turned into powerful illustrations of divine truth. Sometimes the gathering was in a synagogue, but most of the time it was by the sea, in a field, in a garden, on a city street, or by a pool surrounded with the diseased.

The emerging church will likely be less like what it is and more like the above. Appointed programs with performances and entertainment may become a thing of the past in the vital church of tomorrow. Spontaneous testimonies, uncontrolled (by human hand) worship, and gatherings without walls or boundaries will be more frequent.

Small Groups

All across the world, particularly in third-world countries, cell-group churches are springing up and growing quickly to be the largest churches on the planet. These phenomena are emerging in Africa, South America, Korea, Thailand, and yes, even the United States! One of the emerging leaders and gurus of this movement is Ralph Neighbour, who makes his home in Houston, Texas, and Southeast Asia in Singapore. He has preached the gospel of small groups for more than three decades and until recently seemed to be a voice speaking in the wilderness with few listening. This did not deter him. Citing case studies in Korea and around the world, he continued to hammer home his message of the viability of the cell-group church and the diminishing success of the program-based-design church. He is now being heard. He is speaking from the platform of a flourishing cell-group church in Singapore as its associate pastor. He is overseeing the training of hundreds of dedicated, dynamic leaders to staff the cells of the Faith Community Baptist Church that pervade the Garden City of the Orient. His book *Where Do We Go from Here?* is rapidly becoming a standard for cell-group churches. His materials are in great demand, as are his personal services in seminars and conferences across the world.

The cell-group in some form is a virtual necessity as a laboratory for the implementation of the priesthood of the believer. Because the church is the body of Christ her existence is more organic than organizational. In such a church the individual is vital to the normal life of the corporate whole, not just as a technical statistic but as a functioning necessity. In the human body, made up of trillions of cells, there are groups of cells that make up the heart and its functions, the liver and its duties, the pancreas, and all other organs. The human body is a laboratory study in cell life. The church is the body of Christ. A normal and healthy church presupposes that all the organs (cell groupings) are properly functioning in and of themselves as well as in harmony with all the other systems of the body.

If the Church Is the Body of Christ, What Is the Brain?

The president of the United States signed into law a decree designating the decade preceding the twenty-first century the decade of the brain. Millions of dollars are being spent on unprecedented brain research. We are discovering that the brain is a phenomenal organ, not only containing our thought processes but emotional coding which determines our behavior. We are also discovering that the brain is a producer of natural substances which heal illnesses and alleviate pain and that synthetic drugs actually mimic those a healthy brain produces. The human being is no healthier than his or her brain.

With this model before us, what is the brain of the church? Jesus Christ is the head of the church. This not only means that He is its Lord, Master, Boss, and sovereign Leader but its brains. Just as the proper coding of health and behavior is programmed in the healthy brain, so is the health and behavior of the church encoded in the very mind of Christ. It is His body.

The healthy human body must experience constant and thorough communication between the brain and every area of the body. So with the body of Christ must communication with the Head be constant. Any part of the body out of touch with the head is a diseased member. The living Word speaks the Word of God to the body of Christ. This Word is set in print, which forms a standard for all that is said. As man cannot live by bread alone but by every word out of the mouth of God, so the church cannot live by programs and activities but by constant communication with its Head.

In a human body there are thousands of opportunities every few seconds for something to go wrong (or right). Wrong commands coming from the brain or independent action in a cell or cell group may eventuate in serious disruption of the life functions or even death. In the body of Christ there is an absolute necessity of unceasing interfacing with the entire body. Such total communication is sure to result in an alert, aware, and dynamic church.

Vital life signs reflect levels of health in any organism. The church at the turn of the century is sure to have these signs of vitality. The "God-is-dead" movement of the 1960s might have been an honest report on the part of a few who had checked the pulse of their churches and found no heartbeat. Thus, the conclusion seemed in order that since the body was dead, the Head was dead.

We may be dealing now with the "God-is-in-a-coma" movement or at best with the "God-is-anemic" movement. I have been expecting to hear the title of a forthcoming book or movie in line with "Honey, I Shrunk the Kids" to be "Honey, Somebody Shrunk God!"

Comfort with the Supernatural

Up until now the evangelical church in general has maintained a high level of discomfort with the supernatural. In its defense it has been exposed to some unfortunate expressions which have been carried on in the name of the supernatural. It must be remembered that w-e-i-r-d does not spell supernatural. There is a difference between unnatural and supernatural. The latter is often intensely natural, practical, and comfortable. Jesus was intensely natural. He did not have to act religious and thus unnatural. He was SUPER-natural! Folks were drawn to Him, not repelled by Him.

The church will soon become accustomed to visitations of God in which events occur which cannot be explained by natural laws.

After a while they will be accepted and acceptable. We will be more at home in the presence of God and divine activity. We will witness the powerful work of the Spirit and the Word healing, cleansing, enlightening, and empowering, and find ourselves totally unthreatened by it all.

A Turn-of-the-century Awakening?

What a grand day for an awakening! The wellsprings of human resources have dried up before our eyes. Mankind is virtually out of machinations. The experts are fresh out of advice. Our vaunted twentieth century gods are being exposed as fraudulent. The promise of paradise is laid waste. The shrines of power, sex, and money at which this surfeited generation has worshipped are toppling.

Could it be that in its confusion our tormented world will look to the church to see if it might have a word? And might this great body, once weakened by indulgence and compromise, now infused with the power of the Spirit, arise with a certain Word—the Word of God with power—and say, "This is the way, walk in it!"?

Bill Bright is one of the Christian world's greatest visionaries. Almost thirty years ago he said something that is as fixed in my brain today as it was the afternoon I first heard it:

> If we could but show the world that being committed to Christ is no tame, hum-drum, sheltered monotony, but indeed the greatest adventure the human spirit could ever know, the world, now looking askance, would come crowding in to pay allegiance and we could expect the greatest revival since Pentecost.

II believe this with greater intensity at this moment than when I first heard it. Surely the Word of God is the key feature as the Spirit of God acts upon our commitment.

The Christian World in General

A Shift in Bible Study Methods

With the realization that the written Word of God must be illumined by the Holy Spirit who initially inspired it will likely come changes in Bible study.

While most churches claim that the Bible is their sole authority in dogma, most are in fact founded and regulated by a hermeneuti-

cal perspective. Two persons on the same intellectual level may
read the same passage of Scripture and arrive at a totally different
conclusion according to an agenda in hermeneutics (a method of
Bible study). This is very likely to shift. As the cure for pneumaphobia (fear of the Spirit) is experienced, the Holy Spirit will
take center stage in Bible study and interpretation. The value of
background and language study will not diminish, but it will be ac-
centuated by the Word of the Spirit who first breathed it.

This trend is already being noted across the world as new Bible
schools and ministry schools are gaining notice. This is in part a reaction to the totally intellectual and technical approach to the Bible
without emphasis on the Holy Spirit. An unhealthy reaction to biblical scholarship may be apparent at first, but this should be short-
lived as we realize that scholarship and illumination of the Spirit
are not mutually exclusive.

This may, at first reading, be disturbing to the traditional reader,
but I challenge everyone to entertain the following question:
Whose sword is it?

The Bible is God's Word. This means that it not only came from
but it belongs to God. It is His and always will be. Paul called it the
"sword of the Spirit, which is the word of God" (Eph. 6:17). It is
not the seminary's sword or the denomination's sword or even the
individual believer's sword. It does not belong to us to interpret and
use according to our own intellect, regardless of how keen it is. The
sword of the Spirit is for the Spirit's purpose, not ours. We are
given to clubbing each other with our private interpretations of the
Bible, thus deepening the divisions in the body of Christ. In our
hands the Bible is often used as a dull battle-axe to bludgeon each
other senseless. This result is edification for neither of us.

The implications of this truth (that the Bible is the Sword of the
Spirit) has far-reaching significance. It is not our sword; it is His!
We are cautioned against private interpretations of Scripture (2 Pet.
1:20-21). While we may deeply respect biblical scholarship and de-
plore the habits of the unschooled who take large liberties with private interpretations, the fact is that not even the respected scholar
is entitled to a private or provincial interpretation.

If the Bible is God's Word and by His Spirit He breathed it into
existence, He alone has the authority to interpret it. We place the
Bible at its highest level when we put it back into the hands of God.

The highest view of inspiration must contain the present tense work of the Spirit of God upon the Scripture. The Bible did not have its origin in the will of man but holy men spoke as they were "moved by the Holy Ghost" (2 Pet. 1:21). It is, therefore, not consistent to believe that any part of it can be properly interpreted by the unaided human mind.

This may come as a shock, but one of the major implications of this hard truth is that God has the right to change your interpretation of the Scripture at any time He chooses. As we allow God to interpret His own Word in and for us, it comes to life! As we allow Him to work through us in the ministry of the Word, it becomes a two-edged sword in His hands with the precision of a skilled surgeon's scalpel. It quickly cuts to the heart of the matter, exposing and removing all that threatens our spiritual progress.

In any hands other than the One who originally spoke it, the Word of God can be an instrument of division, destruction, and death. In God's possession it is an instrument of light, life, and liberty. Grave dangers always result when a person or group takes possession of the Word of God.

Doctrines, at first issuing from and regulated by the Scriptures, may take on dogmatic and legalistic form and practice and become walls of divisiveness separating God's people. Truth held and practiced as vital in one generation bringing spiritual awakening may in a succeeding generation be a wall of division bringing darkness and death.

The Restoration of Unity

A rediscovery of the Word of God with power is sure to bring the fragments of the body of Christ into closer proximity, thus encouraging cooperation with the Holy Spirit in moving us toward the answer to the prayer of Jesus, "That they may be one" (John 17:22).

For years I have had the privilege of moving and ministering among the varying sections of the body of Christ both in America and throughout the world. On the one hand I am saddened that each is kept from the other by systems of thought and rules of interpretation. But on the other hand, I am excited to discover that these varying sections are beginning to benefit each other by loosening their grip on their own provincial interpretations of Scripture and joining hands for a task that demands our united energies. As this occurs on an increasing scale we will give the Holy Spirit access into our churches, making us candidates for revival.

From the west, men will fear the name of the LORD, and from the rising of the sun, they will revere his glory. For he will come like a pent-up flood that the breath of the LORD drives along. "The Redeemer will come to Zion, to those in Jacob who repent of their sins," declares the LORD. "As for me, this is my covenant with them," says the LORD. "My Spirit, who is on you, and my words that I have put in your mouth will not depart from your mouth, or from the mouths of your children, or from the mouths of their descendants from this time on and forever," says the LORD.

"Arise, shine, for your light has come, and the glory of the LORD rises upon you. See, darkness covers the earth and thick darkness is over the peoples, but the LORD rises upon you and his glory appears over you. Nations will come to your light, and kings to the brightness of your dawn. Lift up your eyes and look about you: All assemble and come to you; your sons come from afar, and your daughters are carried on the arm. Then you will look and be radiant, your heart will throb and swell with joy."

—Isaiah 59:19—60:5, NIV

❧

An Ancient Myth—A Modern Paradigm

We have come to the end of this journey together. Good-byes are always difficult for me. While I know what we say in these delicate times is always important, I am always a bit anxious that the wrong thing might be said or that the most right thing might not be said.

I suggested early on that the reader begin with a glance at these pages. I hope you did and now I trust that you will read them again with a fresh determination to beseech God for a fresh move in the church. From the unlikely source of heathen mythology comes this closing illustration.

Hercules is a well-known figure in Greek mythology. His name has become an adjective describing something requiring great strength. It will help here to recount an episode in the myth of Hercules:

Hercules was among the lesser gods—all of whom were flawed—and, on the occasion of losing his famed temper and slaughtering his wife and children, he was assigned by the superior gods several very difficult tasks as punishment. Among these feats were killing the Nemean lion, taming the Cretan bull, capturing the Cerneian stag, slaughtering the Lernaean hydra (a serpent with nine heads), and securing the magic girdle of Hyppolyte. All were humanly impossible tasks.

By far the most interesting, novel, and difficult task assigned him was that of cleaning the ox stables of King Augeas. This king had three thousand oxen housed in the stables and, because they were especially blessed by the gods, the oxen seemed unaffected by the mounting filth. Thus King Augeas had little interest in cleaning the filthy stables. They had not been cleaned in thirty years! Hercules was assigned the task of cleaning the stables in one day—a Herculean task indeed!

Hercules could have taken a look at that mess and thought within himself, *Wow, this is impossible!*' But, having succeeded in previous tasks, he was not one to give up now. As the story goes, there were two rivers flowing near the stables. Not to be outdone by dung, Hercules made two openings in the stables, front and back, joined the two rivers together, and diverted their course by a channel through the stables. They were cleansed in a single day!

An ancient myth? Yes, but a modern paradigm. The church today is piled high with the dung of meaningless tradition and unbiblical ideas. We have turned our preachers into manure merchants, dung dealers, poo-poo peddlers. The nutrition of yesterday has become the waste of today. Cherished traditions, of great value yesterday, are empty idols today. The treasures of the past have become the trash of the present. Methods, once productive, are revered but useless icons today. That the church needs a cleansing is without debate. The pastors cannot do it alone, nor should such be expected. One after another here and there have tried and all have failed. And the dung piles higher!

Through the world and always near the church flow two mighty rivers—the Spirit and the Word. One (the Spirit) empowers the other (the Word); the other (the Word) provides the channel for the flow of the one (the Spirit). They are both necessary, each complimentary to the other and mutually dependent. One (the Spirit) is the source; the other (the Word) is the course. The flow of each is vital but incomplete without the other.

Some through the years have tapped into the flow of these mighty rivers and felt their power to restore, purify, and enable. At times a whole culture has been caught in the floodtide. But at present it seems that the rivers are so far away and the channels, if any at all, are too small.

If the body of Christ on earth today can dig a channel to these great rivers through humbling repentance and prayer, connecting them with the body, the cleansing will be wonderful, swift, and thorough.

It is toward this fresh rediscovery of the vitality of the living Word of God and the empowering ministry of the Holy Spirit that I present this volume.

Our Lord, mightier than Hercules, waits to accomplish the task! His ultimate design for the church is no secret. He is committed to "make her holy, cleansing her by the washing with water through the word, and to present her to himself a radiant church, without stain or wrinkle or any other blemish" (Eph. 5:26-27, NIV).

Lord, bring the rivers together in the church and let them flow!

&

Endnotes

[1]Jack Rogers, *Biblical Authority* (Waco, Tex.: Word Publishing Co., 1977), 9.

[2]Ibid., 12.

[3]Ibid., 11.

[4]Ibid., 164.

[5]*New Review of Books and Religions* (New York: Seabury Book Service, 1976), 7.

[6]A. W. Tozer, *The Pursuit of God* (Camp Hill, Pa.: Christian Pubns., Inc.), 81-82.

[7]Ibid., 73-74.

[8]Ibid., 74.

[9]Ibid., 75.

[10]W. J. Bauer, paper delivered to a high school class (November 28, 1989), 14.

[11]Ibid.

[12]Tozer, 75.

[13]Watchman Nee, *The Ministry of God's Word* (Richmond, Va.: Christian Fellowship Publishers, 1971), 63-64.

[14]Ibid., 84-85.

[15]Ibid., 86.

[16]Ibid., 87.

[17]Ibid., 92-97.

[18]William Law, *The Power of the Spirit,* compiled by Dave Hunt (Fort Washington, Pa.: Christian Literature Crusade, Inc., 1971), 35-37.

[19]Ibid., 41-46.

[20]Ibid., 56-59.

[21]Ibid., 61.

[22]Eugene Peterson, *Reversed Thunder* (San Francisco: Harper, 1988), 12-15.

[23]Colin Brown, ed., *New International Dictionary of New Testament Theology,* vol. 3 (Grand Rapids, Mich.: Zondervan, 1986), 1078.

[24]Francis Frangipane, *The Three Battlegrounds* (Cedar Rapids, Iowa: Advancing Church Pubns., 1989), 20.